Copyright © 2012 by Sherry Bakhtian

All rights reserved. This book or any portion thereof may not be reproduced or used in any manner whatsoever without the express written permission of the publisher except for the use of brief quotations in a book review as permitted by copyright law.

Printed in the United States of America

First Printing, 2012

ISBN 978-0-9837150-0-9

Bakhtian Creative Solutions

www.icreateaspace.com

bcscoaching@icreateaspace.com

Stripped Down to the Core

A guide for professional, bicultural women seeking to live an authentic life

By Sherry Bakhtian, PhD, ACC

For My Father,

Goshtasb Bakhtian

Contents

Introduction i

SECTION I

Chapter 1: Who Are They, These Amazing Warriors? 1

Chapter 2: What Happened? 15

SECTION II

Chapter 3: Self-Awareness/Self-Observation 29

Chapter 4: Core Values 42

Chapter 5: Big Picture Perspective 53

Chapter 6: Belief Systems 67

Chapter 7: Obstacles 77

Chapter 8: Choice 87

Chapter 9: In It, But Not Of It 95

Chapter 10: Putting It All Together 105

Introduction

The wonderful thing about life's hardships is that they push us forward and force us to grow. We refuse to sit with our hardships, because we naturally want to overcome them. The harder we're pushed, the more we fight back. We find ourselves struggling to find a balance between avoiding situations that we cannot easily overcome, and a healthy desire to overcome the challenges our lives offer. And our perspective changes, too. For example, what may have seemed like a tragedy can work itself out to be the best thing that happened, or even transform into the event that helped shape our future. Later on in life, we may not even recall it as a significant event especially in comparison to what came along later. This is how life is an ever-evolving experience.

The hardships that drive the heroines of this book forward are often caused by their efforts to meet the expectations of people from two different cultures. The balancing act and uncertainties about their identities have driven them into becoming high-achieving individuals, in part to avoid being identified by their place or culture of origin. Mostly however, they just want to be themselves regardless of the color of their skin, accent, and lifestyle choices. These bright, hard-working, and amazingly talented women have chosen education and success as their new identity.

With a fair amount of self-awareness, they are finding themselves more and more asking again the question: Who am I? The first section of this book describes a common range of challenges and opportunities that specifically tend to confront these heroines. This section reveals how similar challenges have shaped the way that you now experience the world if you are a bicultural woman, and how your adaptive skills may not be serving your best interests anymore.

In the second section of the book, I show you how to determine which of these filters you have built without your conscious awareness, and how they may be holding you back from enjoying your life. You will learn to practice simple exercises to overcome these filters and learn to live your life as the person you have always wanted to be; your true self.

In other words, the first section covers the "what" and "how," and the second section covers the "now what."

I hope that this book will remind you that what you think is true might just be an old tape you are listening to in your own head. The tapes are not who you are, but you have learned to identify with the message they keep delivering. Turn off the tapes, and start listening to your own essence and you will then be reacquainted with your SELF. It is the only way to the answer to the question, "Who am I?"

I've written this book partly because I wish I had had these types of conversations or dialogues with myself long ago. After talking to many other bicultural high-achievers, I realized that I belong to a special tribe. What's wonderful about our tribe is the openness with which we have embraced our new or second culture. The bicultural nature of our experience has provided us with opportunities to create new belief systems and ways of being. The bad news is that because we have created or adopted new belief systems and they have worked for us for the most part, we are reluctant to give them up.

This book is about giving up most of what we have held on to for dear life. Life is always providing opportunities for detachment, and somehow we either avoid them or interpret them as a punishment, tragic accident, negative transition, or other less-than-desirable event, without noticing their potential for positive transformation. When we give up or release what is no longer serving us, we feel stripped. Without the false identities and outdated beliefs, we can operate from our core selves. We can finally be our true selves. Stripped down to the core is the way of living consciously.

The concepts in this book also describe how I view the work that I do. It has always been a challenge for me to explain what I do during a spiritual life-coaching session. Finally, after much deliberation, I've decided that the best way to explain what I do is to create the appropriate space and facilitate the conversations that most of us are afraid to have. It's about turning things on their heads so you can see a different perspective. It's about engaging in life in a completely different way.

This book was written with educated, bicultural women as the main protagonists. I had to write a book about what I know best. The mindset of the women representing this book is one of a warrior. Frank McLynn in his book, *Heroes and Villains* (Pegasus Books, LLC, NY, NY 2009) states,

"Trying to penetrate the minds of history's great leaders is something that can be done only gradually and with great patience. But if asked to pin down one essential prerequisite for all successful warriors, I would reply that it is an extraordinary capacity for dealing with simultaneous and accumulated stress."

Mr. McLynn's warriors aren't quite the type of warriors described in this book, but the women I write about are also extraordinary women with great capacity for dealing with simultaneous and accumulated stress. They even seem to thrive under those conditions.

Being one of the protagonists of the book myself, I know too well about the conversations that I never dreamt of having with myself or with another. This book is about the possibility of living life on your own terms. However, in order to do that, you need to understand what you are all about and then decide what those terms might be. Warriors as Mr. McLynn has pointed out are also pitied. Very few have died happily in bed. They have ended up as victims of their warrior ways.

My hope is that the women who have inspired this book can learn to use their conscious choices to not die as warriors, but rather, as fulfilled and happy human beings who lived life on their own terms. I also hope that it will inspire others to leave behind destructive and dissatisfying lifestyles that do not honor the truth within them. The journey now is about going deep within to rediscover the truth, love, and divine in ourselves. With this rediscovery, we can then stop looking, seeking, and striving for something outside. Satiated and "full" of ourselves we can finally live free.

The format of the book is to allow the internal conversation to begin. I start each chapter with a very short story about a bicultural woman who is facing a challenging scenario, and her mindset during the experience—her self-conversation. Then I review the internal filters that led to this mindset, discuss how these filters developed, and how they distort the woman's experience in a manner that ultimately leads to frustration and dissatisfaction.

At the end of each chapter, we will explore how an alternative self-conversation stripped of these artificial filters would create a fresh and authentic experience that is life affirming, and that will help build a new foundation upon which she is free to live life on her own terms.

As you consider this information, you will find exercises and questions that follow the chapter, with room for you to write and explore the original scenario and its more authentic alternative in terms of your own experience.

I like to think of this book as a workbook that will guide you, to loosen up your thoughts, and engage you in a new conversation, *stripped down to the core*. I'll show you how to build a new mindset, and perhaps a new life—the life you have always wanted to live.

SECTION I

CHAPTER 1

Who Are They, These Amazing Warriors?

I want you to get to know the women who have inspired me to write their stories, because I believe that at least part of their experiences will resonate with you. Let's listen in as one of our model warriors speaks to herself in response to a personal situation that many of us face frequently; that of trying—and often failing—to balance family and career:

Another late night in my office and I feel exhausted. I have to finish this report. Brenda, my boss needs it for her ten o'clock meeting tomorrow. She has been good to me and I have to honor her for that. I know I'll be promoted by the end of the year to VP and I'm only 43. That's so exciting! Mom and Dad will be so proud. They had nothing and worked so hard for me to get an education. They never dreamt that I would go so far. I have to finish quickly, so I can go home to Tim and the girls. He has been so good to take care of them every night this week. I know they miss me, but after spending the weekends with them, I get all itchy to get back to work. Here is where I'm needed the most. Tim is better at parenting than I am. I can't be content with cooking and cleaning and reading stories. I am better at taking care of our department and helping out my boss. Even though I am not taking care of my health, no exercise and cancer runs in our family, I have to do this for now. Once I turn 50, I'll slow down. I'll have that next promotion and I will have given my girls the opportunities I never had.

Do you recognize anyone in the story on the previous page? Do you know anyone who might fit into the story? This chapter focuses on the people who have inspired this book. I've tried to capture all possible varieties of people whose story this might be. If you are not interested in the details of "who," then please move on to Section II.

The women in this book are referred to as warriors because of the battles they have fought to get to where they are. Their battles are not as literal as those fought during an actual war, but their experiences are similar in many ways. After winning most of their battles, sometime in the middle of their lives they find themselves deeply dissatisfied and wondering if there is more to it all. What brings them to the realization of their deep, inner dissatisfaction is usually an unexpected change such as the loss of a job, a loved one, a medical diagnosis, or divorce.

These women generally are curious about spirituality and the meaning of life. They wonder if there is a bigger plan and how their lives fit into it. They have had to believe in some greater power, even if they were not brought up in a religious environment, to be able to endure some of the challenges they have had to face. If you are not described in the demographics below, yet you find yourself in the same place as these warriors, please continue reading.

The Demographics

The warrior in this book is somewhere in her mid-thirties to early fifties. She is highly educated, and has earned at least a Master's degree in a traditionally male-dominated field. She is bicultural. She is a professional, working in the stressful corporate world.

She was either born in her adopted country to first generation parents who emigrated from another country for political or economic reasons, and who still speak in their native language and practice their native customs and culture. Her parents may not speak the language of their new country. She may have been born to parents who did not encourage retaining her native language or customs in favor of total integration and even rejection of the native culture. Or she was born in another country and emigrated to the U.S. at a young age for better educational opportunities, and she is at least bi-lingual and practices the customs of her native culture.

Profile

Our warrior has had to face hardships early in life. As a daughter of an immigrant family, the hardship for the family as a whole was most probably financial. They were living paycheck to paycheck, without a sense of security regarding the future, and this fear remains strong in her today.

If the family immigrated for political reasons, they may have been financially secure in their country of origin. Here in their adopted culture, they are waiting for their political situation to change so they can go back home to their country of origin, and they continue to live as visitors in their new culture—as though their stay is only temporary. They live life as if they are on an extended vacation. They are in denial that this is their new home. They live in the past and hope for the future.

The hardships are also related in large part to the heroine's new identity as a bicultural citizen. Her ability to speak the new language of her adopted country may have been the source of ridicule and alienation in school. She may have tried at least twice as hard as her classmates to excel in school. This, in turn, made her even more determined to provide a better opportunity for herself and her future children. Her motivations are drawn from negative experiences. In other words, she does not want to have the life her parents had. She does not want to live the difficult life that she remembers living. She wants a better life for herself and her future family.

If her parents were first-generation immigrants, they did not speak English or have an American education. They probably had menial jobs or started their own business and worked tirelessly to make a living. She does not want this for her own kids. She does not even want this for herself. Therefore, she promises herself that she will obtain an education, a prestigious career, and never let outer circumstances determine the direction of her life. She wants to be in charge of her own success and be wealthy, so that she will have the means to help her own parents and take care of them.

Our protagonist fully realizes that she is fortunate to have this opportunity in the U.S. or any other free and developed Western country. She is free to learn, and to have a career. She does not want anything to get in the way of this opportunity. She owes this to her parents, her friends and family back in her country of origin and all the others who don't have this same opportunity. She is responsible and dependable to a fault.

If she comes from a male-dominated native culture, she is even more determined to make her new life work for her. She owes it to all the other girls who did not make it. She is driven to make the most of her opportunities in her adopted culture where men and women are more equal.

She might even decide that she will not marry a man from her original culture. She may prefer to marry a man from her new culture—one who supports her career and independence. Her husband will be equal to her and they will raise their children together. He will be as educated as she is and won't look down on her or be intimidated by her.

In summary, here are the early factors that shape her into who she is today:

- Political and/or economic instability
- Personal instability (divorce or death in family, etc.)
- Awareness of male/female inequality
- Huge sense of responsibility and loyalty
- Not fitting in (always feeling different from others)
- Dream of a better future through hard work

Personality

Early on...

In her earlier years, she was quiet. She was always studying, working hard to get good grades to make her parents proud and to succeed. Since she didn't have many girlfriends, it was easier for her to take the tough classes with the other boys. They weren't like the typical girls and she could be left alone. The few other girls in her tough classes were nerdy, but serious about school. They didn't mind asking her for help and she didn't mind helping them. Her friendships were based on who was in her classes and who liked taking difficult classes.

She was not afraid of academic challenges. Emotionally, she pushed back her feelings because she was not going to feel sorry for herself. Her tough academic choices made it easier for her to not dwell on the past and she chose to numb her feelings. She had to achieve her academic goals. It was what kept that conversation on mute. She would notice the ones who were always picked on, the ones who were not as good as she was in school, and she was friendly and compassionate toward them. She abhorred injustice and cruelty. She noticed it all the time and made sure she never inflicted it on anyone herself.

The compulsion to prove to everyone that she was equal to, if not better than others had become a natural part of her experience. She became an over-achiever and loved every minute of it, especially since in her mind it guaranteed success and a better life. Success was freedom from lack, ignorance, inequality, or other issues that were personally important to her. Success was also a guarantee of safety. Once she got a taste of it, she kept going back for more.

She may have had softer, more creative interests like art, acting, or literature. She kept them as hobbies and knew better than to think that she could earn a good living as an artist or a history teacher. She became pragmatic. Even if she secretly wanted to be an artist or a dancer, she knew better than to expect her parents to understand this. She believed that they hadn't made the sacrifices they did for her to become a mediocre flute player. They wanted her to have a good job and they didn't think that you could achieve that through art. The conversation about artistic or less pragmatic options never happened and she does not blame anyone for this.

These Days...

Today, she is definitely a type-A personality—demanding, hardworking, critical, and relentless, mostly toward herself. It does however, spill onto those near her. She thinks obsessively about her job, how to do better, how to get to that next level, and she chooses her allies carefully. She will do anything for a first-rate boss. She is loyal, if not to a person, then to an idea. She is someone you can count on. She will get the job done. She might have to stay late every night, but she'll finish what she started. She is honest, and she is courageous, sometimes to a fault.

Her bosses like her, because she exceeds their expectations in her ability to get things done without complaints. She never whines or gives an attitude. She is grateful for her job and they appreciate that.

> **She is a team player, but she usually takes on more than others…and when she decides that she has had enough, she walks away.**

She usually takes on more than others do and then gets annoyed when they aren't working as hard as she is. She internalizes constantly. She over-analyzes situations, and when she decides that she has had enough, she walks away. If she feels like she is being pushed against a wall unjustly, she will have to make a tough choice, like deciding to quit. The decision-making time could take anywhere from days to years.

No one person can make the decision for her; it has to be done by her, and in her own time. She gets very quiet when she is about to make a major decision and she doesn't open up or confide to others during this time. That's why when she does make a move, it usually surprises others.

The following characteristics are fairly typical of the woman described here:

- She is independent.
- She is a detailed thinker.
- She is fair.
- She knows what the rules are and tries her best not to step on any toes.
- She demands a lot from those who work for her, but demands the same, if not more, of herself.
- She'll go to bat for her people and for a boss who she thinks deserves her loyalty.
- She works hard every day.
- She has a strong sense about what is right, and what is not, and she acts and speaks accordingly.

What Drives Her

• Not Fitting In

What pushed her in the beginning was the need to resolve the feeling that she did not belong. Either this awareness could have happened as a result of her being bicultural, or it could have been something deeper. She felt alone, and staying perpetually busy was one way of numbing her feelings of rejection or not belonging. Working hard distracted her from worrying about her parents' conversations about money or other hardships. It kept her focused on breaking free of the life she was currently living.

If only she could get to the next level, achieve the next goal, make more money, or reach whatever standard she deemed as a measure of success, then she would finally be like everyone else or like the select few she admired, or perhaps she wouldn't need anyone anymore. This internal friction of never belonging anywhere was a strong force for change that drove her toward her impressive achievements. Not fitting in provided her with the motivation to seek answers to questions that others did not ask. It drove her to look deeper at herself, her situations, and other people. It enriched her inner life and gifted her with the ability to empathize with others who were experiencing difficulties.

> **This internal friction of never belonging anywhere was a strong force for change that drove her toward her impressive achievements.**

Another gift that one receives from living life as an outsider is the ability to detach and to observe objectively. When you are a bicultural person who has been transplanted from one culture into another, it is natural not to have a myopic view of the world. The fact that she comes from one place and has had to blend into another gives her depth of understanding that is less attached to a single point of view. She is flexible and open towards others as a result.

- Reactivity

The second driving factor is her reactivity. She is not passive and has never been so. If something is not right in her world, she is compelled to correct it. In fact, she is so reactive that the thought of sitting around and waiting for something to happen just makes her sick. Nothing good ever happens on its own. She has to make it happen.

At work, she is the happiest and most productive when she believes in what she is doing. If she is asked to do something that is not right to her, something that will compromise her values, she grows rebellious, stubborn, or uncooperative. She doesn't care if the orders are coming straight from the top—no one can convince her to bend her rules. She will relentlessly try to convince her bosses of her point of view. She is passionate about what she believes in, often to her detriment.

- Action

The third driving factor is her "doing" nature. After her reactivity has been triggered, she feels compelled to take decisive action. She can only rest after she has become completely exhausted from too much activity. She is the one who stays after the dinner parties helping the hostess clean up. She is the one making food for the whole week and freezing it away. She is the one who can always squeeze one more thing on her plate. She craves being busy.

Doing, staying busy, and taking action, makes her feel in control of her life. It also numbs her so that she cannot connect with her heart and truly feel her own emotions. It is probably something she learned as a result of not addressing her transition into a new culture. She has learned to avoid the luxury of feeling her own emotions. It is a defense mechanism that works, because afterwards she is so exhausted that she falls asleep quickly and deeply, with no time left to experience her feelings. The next day it begins all over again.

- Justice

The fourth driving factor is justice. Perhaps this is tied to "not fitting in." She has always been aware of others who are being mistreated, and she goes out of her way to help those who she believes have been stepped on. Even if there is no one person involved, when someone suggests an idea that is unfair, her feathers get ruffled and she gets reactive and plans her next move to either be heard or to effect justice.

What motivates her is a sense of purpose and meaning. Without justice, there is no purpose or meaning. If the establishment treats people unfairly or is blind to those who are truly working hard, then her efforts could also go unnoticed or misinterpreted. Her reactivity is in high gear when she detects injustice.

Because of the factors mentioned in her profile, she also seeks a fair monetary reward for a job well done. It is only later on in her career, when she starts getting tired of battling, that she becomes aware that a positive and happy environment is as important to her as financial compensation. This is especially true because her earlier life may not have been so happy and positive. Working in a peaceful environment is a must these days. She starts the process of re-evaluating her priorities.

- Safety

She craves security. She wants to have X amount of money by a specific time or age, and that number can change. Sometimes the number continues to increase, because she never feels safe and secure. She is always aware of the "fact" that she could lose it all. She is always aware of how things used to be for her and her family when she was younger. She can't go back to that. If she is facing a downsizing at her job, all her old fears come back. If she is contemplating divorce, all her old fears come back.

Review

Let's review her story: *Another late night in my office and I feel exhausted. I have to finish this report. Brenda, my boss needs it for her ten o'clock tomorrow. She has been good to me and I have to honor her for that. I know I'll be promoted by the end of the year, VP and I'm only 43. That's so exciting. Mom and Dad will be so proud. They had nothing and worked so hard for me to get an education. They never dreamt that I would go so far. I have to finish quickly, so I can go home to Tim and the girls. He has been so good to take care of them every night this week. I know they miss me. But after spending the weekends with them, I get all itchy to get back to work. Here is where I'm needed the most. Tim is better at parenting than I am. I can't be content with cooking and cleaning and reading stories. I am better at taking care of our department and helping out my boss. Even though I am not taking care of my health, no exercise and cancer runs in our family, I have to do this for now. Once I turn 50, I'll slow down. I'll have that next promotion and I will have given my girls the opportunities I never had.*

If she were to suddenly learn to turn the old tapes off, below is what she might say upon reflection and self-observation.

The NEW un-filtered conversation might be something like this: I wanted to be in charge of my life, provide a better life for my children, and meet all of my goals. I worked hard to get my education, land a dream job in a good company, make more money than my parents did, marry well, and raise wonderful kids. Now, however, I am a slave to my job. I am a slave to success. I am a slave to my identity. There is no joy in this. It is never enough. I've forgotten who I am or what makes me happy.

This may sound pessimistic, but it is realistic. And when we gain a bigger perspective and can see more of what is actually in front of us, we can begin to grow and change in a manner that is life affirming and joyous.

Now, relax and take a few deep breaths. The exercises below are meant to take your experience of the words in this chapter to a deeper level. Please take the time to write down your answers. You can use a journal if you prefer. Don't worry about what you are writing; let it come out as naturally as possible without worrying about grammar, sentence structure, or length of your paragraphs.

Exercise:

1. After reading about our protagonist's experiences and how they shaped her reactions to life, do you feel as though you resemble her in some ways?
2. In what ways are you the same?
3. In what ways are you different?
4. Do you relate to being a soldier or a warrior? How does that analogy make you feel? Explain.

CHAPTER 2

What Happened?

...So I bought my mom a beautiful designer handbag. It cost me a bundle, but it was for Mother's Day and I certainly can afford it. You know, after all that she and dad have done for us, I figured, it is about time I showed her how much I appreciated it. Well, it has been three months and I still haven't seen her carry it or use it. So I asked why she won't use the bag, and she tells me it's because it doesn't go with anything she has and she feels like she's bragging to her friends if she carries it around. Then she proceeds to tell me that I shouldn't have spent so much money on it, that I could have bought her a whole outfit and a new department store purse with that much money. No matter how hard I try, they just won't accept any expensive gifts. They can't enjoy the luxuries that money provides. They still worry about money and it drives me nuts.

I have money, but I still think about having more. I can't seem to enjoy spending it on my parents because of their reaction to the gifts I buy them. There is always a part of me that is worried that I might not have enough. Even though I spend my money, I still worry. I am tired of working so hard. The kids are getting older and are starting to complain that I am never around or happy. I am always obsessing about work...

Even though the bicultural warriors in this book may have integrated with their new culture, they retain their unique story—a story that needs to be told.

Like the pilgrims who came to America in the 1700s, their story is one of struggle, focus, determination, and extreme hard work. They are the ones their families counted on; they are the ones who built a new life in a new land. They wanted to take advantage of all that their parents could not have had, such as an education, freedom, and self-made material success. This part of their journey cannot be minimized; it is the main force that determined the trajectory of their path.

What makes these women different from their parents though, is that on some level they are being pushed to integrate into a new culture. Their success depends upon how well integrated they are. If they are looked upon by others as an Eastern European, Middle-Eastern, Asian, or whatever their culture of origin, they might be discriminated against. So they have all found a way to integrate. Some have done this seamlessly, while some are still outwardly struggling. All are torn inside. At best, they are neither one nor the other; they are a tribe or culture unto themselves.

These are the reasons for their intense spiritual curiosity, which is an inherent component of this profile. When a deep sense of not belonging defines your experience of life, you become curious about who you are. If you are not an Eastern European, Middle Eastern, Asian, or an American, what does it all mean? How does your life fit into it all? And if you do not fit, then what?

History/Story

We know that our protagonist is bicultural and that she started out by feeling as if she did not belong. She had a challenging childhood. Her anxiety about money and her strong desire for a sense of security followed her, and continues to haunt her today. In fact, when you ask her why she works so hard, she mentions her parents and their story and how she does not want to suffer as they did. This is the running headline in her head, which keeps her plodding the same weary distance on the same treadmill every day. As fast and as far as she thinks she is running, there are still threads pulling her back into the story of her ancestors and where she came from.

If she has children, another story that she internalizes is that she is responsible for her children's welfare and education. She works hard to provide for them. It is what her parents did for her. The fact that she is never around or she is emotionally and mentally unavailable, even when she is sitting on the couch next to them, is not sufficient reason to stop working so hard and obsessing about work at the end of the day. Her husband either is doing the same or is nagging about her unavailability. This causes a lot of tension in their marriage. The kids are getting to be more demanding. She is tired and stressed and she does not feel any romantic connections with her husband or significant other.

She may even be a single mom, which brings her pain more clearly into view. Without another consistent person to share the responsibilities of parenting, she feels pushed against the wall with nowhere to go but work. Her running headline is, *"Just keep working, it will pay off. When you make that next promotion, you'll have more money to finally take the vacation you promised your child, hire a nanny, save for college, and more."*

She is a master at justifying her addiction to work; an attitude she either directly inherited from her parents or conversely adopted to avoid becoming too much like her parents.

She is approaching mid-life or is there already. She is aware of all that this means. Her mortality is in clear view. She is concerned about the way she looks, she has gained some weight and has no time to exercise or to eat right, and food is her only comfort. She used to look so good and she wonders what happened. She finds that self-care tasks such as coloring her hair or getting a haircut are the only pampering she allows herself. She does spend money on clothes from time to time, especially when she gets her bonus check, because she feels entitled to owning quality possessions. And this is the way she thinks she is different from her parents.

She spends her money on what her parents would consider frivolous things, because she never had any frivolous things when she was growing up. She is making up for all that she never had. She wants to know what it feels like to buy designer shoes.

Her husband used to buy her special gifts, but they have lost that touch. He doesn't pay attention to her, and he doesn't even know how much money she spends on things. He merely asks her what she wants for her birthday, and she tells him exactly what to buy. There are no more surprises in their lives. They are like roommates sharing the responsibility of the house and their kids.

> **She is making up for all that she never had. She wants to know what it feels like to buy designer shoes.**

Our protagonist is concerned about her own moods. Is she depressed? Is it pre-menopause? Is it stress? She won't speak of these things to others, because she thinks they wouldn't understand. She goes for her yearly check-ups and everything is normal, so she is relieved after every appointment. She tells herself that this must be normal at her age. She tells herself that this is the price of success, or perhaps she is just getting older. No matter, it will all pay off one day.

This elusive magical day that she so diligently works toward is the day when she knows she has *enough*. On this day, she finally won't have to work so hard. She won't have to apologize to her kids and family for missing dinner or a special event at school. She will make it easy for them to have things and they'll forgive her. Everything will be okay on this magical day, or so she dreams.

Oddly enough, our heroine has found that vacations are actually more stressful than going to work. Vacations require her to spend time with her family, and they drive her nuts. She wants to not be in charge. She wants to be taken care of and left alone, but her family wants her attention. She has no patience and she doesn't find theme parks or holiday resorts amusing. She and her family end up spending far too much money and not enjoying any of the time that flies by so quickly. When she returns to work after a vacation, she is relieved to be back on comfortable ground, where she can be in control and continue to pursue her goals.

She is on the verge of falling apart any day now.

Help

Even though our model is not happy or satisfied with the quality of her life, and she may even be having trouble at work, she is determined to maintain the status quo. She believes that counseling and therapy are for weak people with mental problems. She obviously does not have emotional problems, or how could she have finished school, earned all her degrees, and successfully kept her career going? She does not talk about her problems with anyone, mainly because she does not let anyone get too close to her. Sometimes she does not even know what she would share. Everyone thinks that she has it all, so how could she shatter their fantasies? She keeps on telling herself that once the kids are older it will be easier, or this is what she is thinking as she fastens her seatbelt for yet another ride through her dissatisfying and exhausting, but "successful" life.

What she may not realize yet is that for every woman who fits this model and serves in this role, something drastic and unexpected usually happens to throw this sick ride off the tracks.

But what could be serious enough to derail her?

- Failure of her marriage (husband requesting a divorce, having an affair, or finding out about hers)
- Death of a parent, sibling, or child
- Serious work issue (Losing her job or being demoted from her position)
- Trouble with kids (kids getting seriously ill, having problems at school, etc.)
- Serious health issue (diagnosed with cancer, sustaining permanent injuries from an accident, chronic pain, or other impairment)

The only way she'll ask for help is if she is somehow derailed from her path, and derailment is inevitable when she remains stubbornly and willfully driven to attain more and more success. Success—as she defines it—is the purpose of every breath she takes, and yet she either is not aware of this obsession, or she is in denial. Success to her is the promise of control over her life. Success is all about creating a sense of safety, because she has never felt truly safe. Yet she cannot see what is obvious to outsiders: In this primal quest for success, control, and safety, she still feels "not good enough." She secretly feels she has lost all control, and she rarely feels safe.

Common Issue(s)

- Denial

Usually, our protagonist accepts hard facts, whether it is a boss who just threw her under the bus, or a son who has been diagnosed with learning disabilities. She is extremely levelheaded, responsible, and intelligent, so she won't complain. She states the problem(s) without showing any real emotions. She even takes responsibility for her role in them. If there is any grief about a loss, she declares (and believes) that she is over it, and now she just wants things to go back to normal.

Whatever the case may be, she is in denial because she is approaching the issue with her logical mind and discounting her emotions. She has always approached life and its challenges from her intellect and not her heart. There is no point in feeling badly. She just wants to go into "fix it" mode. She has a plan and she is open to anyone else who may offer her a better plan to get back on track. She is a realist, she tells herself. Her tears are for herself alone, when no one else can see her crying.

- Control Issues

Because her life feels out of control, she tries to direct every situation in her life as much as possible. She is often dissatisfied with her husband and/or family and the quality of their assistance. She is frustrated with her kids, because she believes that she is sacrificing to provide opportunities for them that they do not even seem to appreciate. She is angry with anyone who does not deliver on what they have promised. She always evaluates things and sees what didn't get done or what could have been done better. She comes across to others as a control freak.

- Guilt

She feels guilty if she realizes that she has become a control freak and is not fun to be with. She feels guilty if she loses a loved one, because she knows she failed to be there for them. She feels guilty if her daughter is having problems at school because she wasn't there for her. She feels guilty for having an affair and destroying her marriage and her children's future. She feels guilty for staying in a bad marriage and ruining her children's childhoods with parental tension and strife. Everything that she has not done well, or has not done at all, comes into focus and she secretly hates herself for all that she has failed to do well.

- Obsession About Work

Growing ever more obsessed about work, she continually chides herself that she must do well to hold it all together. She needs the money more than ever, or so she fools herself into thinking. The reality is that work keeps her distracted and she is good at it; she has to be good at her work so that she can continue to feel successful when the rest of her life is crumbling around her.

If she loses her job, she must replace it immediately. Her efforts go into networking and job searching. She panics. Even when she is not at work or looking for work, she is obsessing and reviewing every detail of her hunt, re-analyzing her resume, her conversations, the people she works with, and so on. She is even more on edge than before and everyone close to her recognizes this and worries about her. She ignores them and perseveres.

- Exhaustion

She is now bone-weary. She is mentally tired of holding it all together for too long. She wants to run away and never come back. She fantasizes about it. She is exhausted from all of her responsibilities, resentful of all the people who are demanding things from her, and she wonders why her life is so complicated. She has forgotten that because she is not available, she has hired people to manage the tasks for which she was too busy, and all of these people must be managed. She yearns for peace and simplicity. She yearns for easier times, when she was only responsible for herself. What has she done? How did it get this way? She doesn't want it to end like this.

What Does She Want?

Here is a sampling of what she says she wants:

- A Simpler Life

She says she wants her life to be simpler, to be more present in the moment with her children, or to have more time for herself.

- Time For Exercise

She says she has no time for physical exercise. She works, and then she is with her kids, helping with homework, cooking and eating dinner, and then she is exhausted. Weekends are filled with grocery shopping, cleaning, or catching up with family, and random, menial tasks.

- A New Relationship

If her marriage is over, she is looking for someone. But where would she find a man her age who would like who she is? How would they meet? There is no time for dating and no pool of available men that she is aware of. If her marriage is still alive, she longs to revamp it and go back to where they first began.

- Peace

She says she wants peace. She is tired of being gnawed at both at work and at home. She wants to recharge by being left alone to read a book, take a long bath, or pick up an old hobby. She wants to chill by herself, to emerge fresh and energized to be around others.

In other words, she says she wants things that she is not truly prepared to have. Her job takes priority over everything. Her marital status is, "married to my job and everything else comes next." With her job taking 10 to 12 hours of her day, not including all the business trips, she does not have time for exercise, kids, a new relationship, or even peace.

Other people work the same hours that she does, but they seem to be able to turn it off at the end of the day, or to not be so totally engaged and working the entire day that they are completely drained by the time they get home. In other words, you don't have to obsess about work 24/7 as she does. But what is she supposed to do? This is simply who she is.

Review

Let's revisit the story again: ... *So I bought my mom a beautiful designer handbag. It cost me a bundle, but it was for Mother's Day and I certainly can afford it. You know, after all that she and dad have done for us, I figured, it is about time I showed her how much I appreciated it. Well, it has been three months and I still haven't seen her carry it or use it. So I asked why she won't use the bag. She tells me it's because it doesn't go with anything she has and she feels like she's bragging to her friends if she carries it around. Then she proceeds to tell me that I shouldn't have spent so much money on it, that I could have bought her a whole outfit and a new designer purse with that much money. No matter how hard I try, they just won't accept any expensive gifts. They can't enjoy the luxuries that money provides. They still worry about money and it drives me nuts.*

I have money, but I still think about having more. I can't seem to enjoy spending it on my parents because of their reaction to the gifts I buy them. There is always a part of me that is worried that I might not have enough. Even though, I spend my money, I still worry. I am tired of working so hard. The kids are getting older and are starting to complain that I am never around or happy. I am always obsessing about work...

Here is the NEW Un-filtered Conversation: *I wanted to make enough money to spend it without worry. Mom and Dad never wanted to spend it. We were different. Our stories intertwined as they always do with intimate relationships, but ultimately, my definition of success and my mindset are different from theirs. I cannot control them or anyone else. I am not responsible for their happiness or anyone else's. I need to remember how to be happy again. Success and money do not make me feel happy,* *in control, or safe. When I last remember feeling those feelings, I wasn't successful; I didn't have much money, and no responsibilities. I also wasn't worried about all the things I worry about today.*

Now, please take a moment to relax and draw a few deep breaths before you start the exercises below. Be honest with your answers and feel free to write in your own journal if you prefer. Let the answers come to you without any filtering or judgment.

Exercise:

1. When was the last time you allowed yourself to receive (e.g., kindness, a gift without having to give back, accepting whatever someone is giving you, and so forth.)? How did it feel? What gets in the way of your receiving?
2. If you have been derailed, what was it that derailed you? How are you handling it? Who is helping you?
3. What do you want? Can you have what you want given the choices you keep making?
4. What would have to change for you to have what you really want?

SECTION II

CHAPTER 3

Self-Awareness/Self-Observation

She was in second grade and she dreaded the holidays. The holidays meant that she would go with her mother and two older sisters to their work. Their work was cleaning rich people's homes. She would follow her mother and look at her feet hoping that the homeowners weren't home and wouldn't look at her. If they weren't home, she'd quietly go to the family room, turn on the giant screen TV, and watch her favorite shows. She'd pretend it was her home and her TV. She'd drift off in her daydreams when she'd hear the vacuum cleaner and her mother arguing with her sister about not doing a good job with the dusting. She promised herself that one day, after she finished school, she'd get a real good job and provide for her mother and sisters, so they wouldn't ever have to clean another person's house.

After all, unlike her mother and sisters, she was born in America, and as an American, she could do anything she wanted someday. She'd live in a house bigger than the ones her mother cleaned. She'd send her kids to nice schools and buy them pretty new dresses and shoes. They'd never wear hand-me-downs. They'd never worry about having to go back to their own country...

Something happened. The rug was pulled from under her and she is now questioning everything. It is the ideal opportunity to start living a bigger life. A bigger life is not necessarily about a bigger house, more money, or a better job, but she is still on the path to learning that. She has been shaken and stirred, and she is slowly beginning to awaken.

Let's go back to the beginning of her story: A bicultural person by definition has had an intimate relationship with profound change. The strength of her family's ties to their original culture determines how tightly she clings to the edge of that change. Some never leave the edge. The edge is what splits her experiences in two. There is the original cultural experience or self-identity, and then there is the adopted culture's self-identity. She may consciously desire to blend the two, but her parents may be resentful of losing their daughter to this new place and customs, and they may clutch at her to pull her back.

Another, opposite scenario may be at play, where her parents are instead enamored with, and appreciative of their new culture—so much so they do not even want her to speak in their language of origin, and they eagerly embrace local holidays and traditions. They may want their daughter to be fully entrenched and integrated into the new culture. In this scenario, she wakes up some time in the middle of her life after the rug has been pulled by a traumatic event, wondering who she really is, and the quest for true self-identity begins.

No matter what her bicultural situation is, the change or the event that defined her as bicultural must be addressed by her adult self. Also, the transition that she may or may not have allowed herself to experience as a result of this change must be processed. After all, you don't wake up one day being an American or a Japanese person, no matter how hard you try. You may learn to speak the language without any accents, learn all the idiomatic expressions, dress the way your peers do, and yet never belong because of the distance you feel inside. That distance needs to be honored and acknowledged for true and complete integration to happen.

This chapter discusses the tool of self-awareness as the first step in this process. Another tool is *"big-picture perspective"* thinking, which is discussed in Chapter 5.

Taking the First Step

- Be still and observe yourself

Most of us are not aware of what drives us to do, say, or even think certain thoughts. We are at the end of the eight-ball being pushed or compelled to go or to do things without realizing who or what drove us there. Worse yet, if asked where the thought came from, we will take ownership as if we were the source of the thought. Only when we are still and observe ourselves (our thoughts, deeds, and words) can we recognize patterns that might give us a clue as to why we do what we do. And then we tend to be surprised at where these thoughts came from.

This all sounds simple, yet it is extremely difficult for the high-achieving corporate mover and shaker. Her world is about actions that produce results. Her world is not about sitting still and observing. In fact, she looks down upon those who are considered "disengaged" because they are judged weak and ineffective, yet she fails to realize that she would be authentically engaged if she would stop to observe what is pulling her strings or motivating her. Then she could consciously choose whether she actually wants to say or do the things that she is saying and doing.

The first step toward real change is objective observation and understanding. If you don't know what the truth is, you cannot make any substantive changes. The truth lies somewhere under all the stories and beliefs we have been fed and continue to feed on. For example, consider the Christmas story of Jesus being born on

December 25 in a manger in Bethlehem. If you are only looking at the tale from the story level, you may believe all the so-called facts, such as the notion that Jesus' birthday is December 25 and that he was born to a virgin in a manger. If you look beyond the story, you will see the challenges of his birth and the impossibility of the world he was being born into, regardless of whether it was on December 25, in Bethlehem, to a virgin, or in a manger.

Society as a whole takes these beliefs at face value, despite the fact that they are derived from a blend of religious scripture—translated several times over—and ancient, man-made customs designed to establish peace between warring factions. Yet we tend to hand these truisms down verbatim to our children without examining our own reasons for our beliefs.

Another example of a common belief that has become truth to many is the belief that "no pain, no gain." In other words, you have to work to the point of physical or emotional exhaustion to make any progress. How did this become a truism? Perhaps someone was trying to teach their child the value of working or trying to get them to help around the house. They encouraged him to work hard by promising him that he'd get something in return, such as a piece of candy or an allowance. The child grew up, this memory stuck in his mind, and he repeated it to his children, and so on. Centuries later, we have a very strong belief system that is based on some truth, but is held within our inner beliefs as an indisputable fact.

While it is a common belief that hard work is required of anyone who wants to succeed in life, the truth is that we all know people who haven't done much and yet have received abundantly. We all know of the person who stayed out of trouble by never saying anything at meetings, or who never met commitments, but who unexpectedly won a promotion despite their lack of work ethic. No pain, no gain? Really?

Awareness and self-observation help to dispel the beliefs that no longer serve us. If all we achieve through increased self-awareness is to loosen the grip that a given truism is a universal fact, then it is worth pursuing. Awareness and self-observation provide the necessary space to re-evaluate and determine what the truth is and what it is not. They provide a space for detachment from ego, because ego is also a culprit in hiding the truth.

> **Centuries later, we have a very strong belief system that is based on some truth, but is held within our inner beliefs as an indisputable fact.**

The most common way we get hurt by our outdated belief systems is when they don't make sense or contribute value to our lives anymore. When you notice discrepancies in your belief systems or an increase in the number of times that you realize they are not true, it is time to let them go. When we live hiding behind our belief systems and away from the truth, eventually we are forced to let go. That is what manifests itself as being fired, getting sick, or being betrayed by someone we trusted.

Why is Self-observation Important?

The only way you can make real change is to recognize the source of the issue. If you are working at the level of effect, then you are only changing the symptoms. True healing begins only when the cause of the disease is resolved. Relieving symptoms is comforting, yet deceiving. Over time, when we hit another wall or are faced with a challenge, the symptoms return because the root cause was not treated.

Symptoms manifest in physical form, too. Studies of subjects with multiple personality disorder have shown repeatedly that one human being can exhibit remarkably different physical responses to disease and physical dysfunction depending on which personality was dominant at the time of testing. For example, one patient had a single personality with diabetes, while her others did not have the disease.[1] Other multiples demonstrate strong allergies or significant vision changes, depending on which of their personalities are manifesting.

Take the example of asthma. These days asthma is treated with wonderful drugs that enable the patient to breathe easier without gasping for air. If you look at the etiology which confirms that the airways are inflamed because of (allergies, bronchitis, or other irritant), and that commonly are thought to cause asthma, you are looking again at the Christmas story and all of its details or so-called facts. Asthma prevents the patient from breathing normally.

What does that mean? Something is causing her such discomfort that she is unable to breathe, and breathing is necessary for life to continue. The trigger could be fear, allergens, an infection, guilt, unhappiness, anxiety, or stress. Chances are that if you helped the patient address the true source of their problem, their asthma would gradually go away. However, most people believe that they can't change certain things in their lives, so their condition continues and is under control with medication that treats the constricted airways.

Self-observation is important because you are the one who can diagnose what is really going on. You are the only one who knows your whole story and all of your beliefs. You are the only one who knows all your own secrets and hidden thoughts. You just don't know them as such. Self-observation allows the invisible to become visible. It is a powerful tool that, like a magnifying glass, can bring focus on the stuff that doesn't serve you, but detracts from the life you want to live.

Self-observation also numbs the pain a bit. When you are observing yourself, you are the audience, and not a participant. The more time you spend being in the audience of your own show, the more detached you become from the drama and the more free you are now to make decisions instead of knee-jerk reacting.

How?

- Practice

The only way to learn how to detach objectively is to practice. Observe yourself in all situations. Start by doing it when you are alone in your car for example. Ask yourself, "What is going on? Am I content? Am I anxious about something? What are the stress-producing events, people, or situations in my life? What are the patterns? Am I most anxious in the mornings or as the day goes on?"

A journal is an important tool to use during self-observation. Write down whatever comes to mind. Let it all come out on paper, so you can finally be still. Being still is not necessarily being still as in meditation. Being still in action is being mindful. You can be mindful doing the simplest and most normal things in the day.

Real change involves reconnecting with source, or our core. It may sound airy-fairy, but it is challenging work that does not require you to climb a mountain and sit in solitude for months unless you want to. Real change can happen in the "real" world. In fact, it must happen in the so-called real world for it to be recognized as real and not airy-fairy. This is how we change the world we live in.

- Breathe

> **Conscious breathing, together with self-awareness, is essential to making the invisible visible to our unseeing eyes.**

Now be still for a moment and simply breathe. Notice your breathing. When you notice how shallow or deep each breath is, then you can decide to change it. Usually we tend to make our breaths deeper when we notice that they are shallow, and normal breathing for most people usually is too shallow. Take a conscious breath, and make it a habit to do so. Conscious breathing, together with self-awareness, is essential to making the invisible visible to our unseeing eyes.

When you become aware of a belief that is causing you anxiety, don't try to fix it. Just breathe it in. Breathe with acceptance of all that is. You are not trying to change anything yet. You are just observing, allowing, and being present with it. When you practice it enough times alone, you can try it when you are in the presence of others. Observe without judging. Notice whether you are bothered by others, whether you are annoyed by something in the environment, and simply breathe it in. Accept and allow.

Notice whether you are annoyed at observing your annoyance! Breathe it in. We tend to resist what bothers us, and in this case, you are being asked to bring it in even deeper. As counter-intuitive as it sounds, this is how we truly face our demons. They are only demons because we have not faced them yet.

As Pema Chödrön, an American Buddhist nun teaches in her book, *Start Where You Are*: *"…When anything is painful, or undesirable, breathe it in. That's another way of saying you are not resisting it. You surrender to yourself, you acknowledge who you are, you honor yourself."*

- Observe

Be an observer of yourself, and learn to notice when you are evaluating a situation. Evaluation soon leads into judgment. Judgment is the child of duality. Judgment requires something to be right and something to be wrong. Condemnation soon follows judgment, and that's when we start feeling self-righteous. Self-righteousness is an addiction. It also triggers control issues. Once you feel self-righteous, then you need to tell everyone what to do because no one knows how to do it the right way! It is a pattern that we keep falling into because we keep evaluating situations. That's what our brain keeps on telling us to do.

Go back to breathing and to self-awareness. If you are unhappy, ask yourself whether it is a result of self-righteousness, or whether you are seeking justice for yourself, someone else, or a cause? Either way, you are unhappy. Breathe it in and take note of it.

- Journal

Your best tool during the practice of self-observation is your journal. If you don't have a journal, you might want to get one. The purpose of keeping a journal is not to write a literary masterpiece. It is simply a tool, and a powerful one. It is a repository for all the thoughts that you don't know what to do with. It helps in processing information. At times, you might find that when you are writing freestyle, stuff gets loosened up much faster.

You might start forming ideas, reach conclusions, and experience sudden "aha" moments while you are writing. Julia Cameron (novelist, playwright, songwriter, poet, and author of, *The Artist's Way*), recommends to write first thing in the morning, and I have found that exercise to be very helpful. It really helps set the day with the intention that you are open.

What happens with time and practice, conscious breathing, awareness of evaluation, and journaling is that you start feeling detached from all the small things and some of the big things that seemed to have bothered you in the past. You become more accepting of others, of different thoughts or situations, and life will seem bigger than it used to be. This is a wonderful feeling that draws you closer to living a masterful life.

---

[1]*New York Times, New Focus on Multiple Personality,* By Daniel Goleman, Published: May 21, 1985, online: http://www.nytimes.com/1985/05/21/science/new-focus-on-multiple-personality.html

Review

Let's revisit the story: *She was in second grade and she dreaded the holidays. The holidays meant that she went with her mother and two older sisters to their work. Their work was cleaning rich people's homes. She would follow her mother and look at her feet hoping that the homeowners weren't home and wouldn't look at her. If they weren't home, she'd quietly go to the family room, turn on the giant screen TV, and watch her favorite shows. She'd pretend it was her home and her TV. She'd drift off in her daydreams when she'd hear the vacuum cleaner and her mother arguing with her sister about not doing a good job with the dusting. She promised herself that one day, after she finished school, she'd get a real good job and provide for her mother and sisters, so they wouldn't ever have to clean another person's house.*

After all, unlike her mother and sisters, she was born in America and as an American, she could do anything she wanted. She'd live in a house bigger than the ones her mother cleaned. She'd send her kids to nice schools and buy them pretty new dresses and shoes. They'd never wear hand-me-downs. They'd never worry about having to go back to their own country...

The NEW Un-Filtered Conversation: *I was determined to succeed, partly because of the shame I felt. My visceral drive to pull my family out of the place they were in had blinded me to the fact that I lived in a place where my dream was a possibility. In fact, sitting in other rich people's homes gave me the blueprint for what I could have for myself. I wish I could see it that way instead of always being embarrassed by where I came from. If I had only stopped running to or from wherever I happened to be, I might have actually enjoyed the scenery.*

Once again, please take a moment to absorb what you have read. Take a few breaths and when you have un-interrupted time to yourself, get your journal and write your unfiltered answers to the following questions. Let the answers take you where they may. Don't evaluate or judge. Just allow and play.

Exercise:

1. What are you judgmental about? Write about it in your journal.
2. What does being judgmental about it get you, in other words, what do you get from thinking these thoughts? What's the benefit to you?
3. What other things do you get all "judgy" about? Write about it in your journal.
4. What would your life be like if you didn't care about these issues?

CHAPTER 4

Core Values

After yet another good performance review, she left his office feeling unappreciated and undervalued. She sat at her desk not understanding why she didn't get the promotion she thought she deserved. She had met all of her goals and achieved them efficiently to his surprise. Yet he seemed to be grasping for words of praise during her review. She couldn't understand why others were promoted before her. They had not achieved as much and were not as hard working as she was, and yet they were being rewarded far more than she was. She remembered him saying, "You need to speak up more in meetings." But the meetings that he wanted her to speak up at were for VPs and above. She was only a manager and she did not think it was appropriate to speak up when the higher-ups were there, especially if she disagreed with them. Besides, she had to do more fact checking before forming an opinion. It would be disrespectful and shameful if she said something that wasn't true...

Without an understanding of what your core values are, it is hard to live by them. Once you know what they are, you might learn that your work or your spouse do not honor your values. In fact, at times you might discover that you are being expected to go against your core values. This discovery will give you an understanding of why you are unhappy when others are not. Once you have clarity about what is truly and inherently important to you, you can make choices to walk away from situations and people that do not honor you.

It is important to not try to convince others of the importance of your values or get them to convert. What is important to you may or may not be important to someone else, and it cannot become so just because you want it to. It does not make them a bad person. For example, if honesty is a core value for you and it isn't for your boss, it doesn't mean that she is a liar. It just means that she does not see life through the lens of truth or lies, she might see a whole other range of possibilities that you are not comfortable with. Furthermore, if your job requires you to consistently play in the range of those possibilities, it may be time for you to leave.

What Are Values?

In a recent workshop, I asked the attendees to write down their top three values, and one person needed clarification because she wasn't sure what a value was. This was not surprising to me. Most people do not know what their values are, or they might believe that something is of the greatest importance to them until someone mentions something else and puts things into perspective for them. The way I define core values are those things we value to the point of "we can't live without them" and we are not sure why or when they became so. In fact, certain core values are so much a part of who we are that we may not even recognize them as values.

Most of the highly educated professional bicultural women I work with tell me that their top three values are justice, freedom, and peace. From the time they can remember, they have been upset by injustice. They like to think of themselves as being fair and they expect others to be the same. When they see injustice or feel like they have been treated unjustly, they are deeply upset. They also need to be allowed the freedom to make their own decisions. Micromanaging supervisors can choke off creativity and passion in such individuals. Peace is a condition that they strive toward continually. When they arrive home after a long day at work, they want peace. Having a peaceful home life is essential to them. When there is discord, fighting, or simply too much noise, they are deeply dissatisfied.

Other values are love, compassion, respect (like the story at the beginning of this chapter), kindness, beauty, courage, and honesty.

Core vs. Outer Values

Certain values are those we pick up based on the cultures we have adapted to. For example, hard work is an American cultural value passed down from the Puritans. This may not be your core value, but because you've seen it in your parents, and everywhere in society and the mass media, you might believe that it is your core value. Another value that can be mislabeled as a core value is courage. If you have had a difficult life, having to stand up for your beliefs and fight against the odds to make your life work, your outer value is courage. It is the value you had to adopt to succeed. It is not a natural part of who you are. You don't like questioning things or standing up for your rights, because it doesn't feel natural. In this case, courage is not a core value, but an outer or adopted value.

> **Hard work is an American cultural value. This may not be your core value, but because you've seen it in your parents, society, and the mass media, you might believe that it is your core value.**

Most people, like the warriors who have inspired this book, have faced difficult circumstances they've been forced to overcome. Their circumstances required them to adopt many outer values for coping and surviving purposes. When you ask them what their top three values are, if they understand the definition of the word, they have a very hard time boiling it down to three. That is due to lack of differentiation between core values and outer values. Sometimes it is hard to tell the difference, especially if the life circumstances have been particularly difficult, or if they are of an extremely sensitive nature.

Outer values generally don't evoke positive memories or feelings. Outer values, at best, inspire logical self-statements, such as, "Well, I had to be strong to endure my situation." In some cases, they provoke a negative response such as, "I am so tired of being brave. I just want to have it easy for a change." Core values are recognized as positive, such as when we tell ourselves, "When I am surrounded by beauty, I feel like I am in heaven," or, "When I am allowed the freedom to do as I please, I am at my most creative, and I feel wonderful when I complete my projects."

Outer values, when recognized, elicit powerful negative emotions, such as sadness and regret. Core values on the other hand, will prompt tears of joy when discussed. Core values describe who you are and have always been. Outer values describe who you have to pretend to be in order to survive.

What to Do With Outer Values?

When you recognize which of your values are core values, and which are outer values, you can choose to create a life in which your core values are expressed consistently. You may realize that you are currently surrounded by your outer values, because those are the values you have adopted so that you could survive. At times, outer values feel like weapons or shields against presumed attack.

You may find that even thinking about or exploring your core values feels foreign, or like a luxury that you are not sure you deserve. Complete satisfaction can only be yours if you are living out your core values. The more you live your core values, the more comfortable you'll feel with releasing yourself from your outer values if you so choose. Although your outer values have served you well, continuing to cling to them implies identifying with them, and you can get lost in that. The path to self-mastery is about stripping down to your essence—your core—and is not about identifying with ideas and concepts that only serve to make you feel safe and protected.

Worse yet, over-identifying with outer values makes us self-righteous. Take the example of the church volunteer who complains about church members who seldom come to church, or who never volunteer to help with cleaning up and other menial tasks. This person may be using her outer value of hard work or helpfulness to justify her self-righteous judgment of those who don't do as she does. If she truly loved volunteering and enjoyed the sense of community that results from working with other like-minded people, she would not be complaining and judging.

This same person might be surprised to recognize that working hard is not her inner value. Upon this realization, she may then re-evaluate her reasons for volunteering. Does she enjoy the work? Is it important for her to help clean up the church? If there is no joy in the work she is doing, then she may want to reconsider her role in the church. We all tend to blame others for our own unhappiness, when indeed the answer is always within us. If we are not being true to who we really are, that is always the source of our unhappiness.

What is one to do with outer values? As mentioned earlier, they were created as a coping mechanism. They are learned survival skills, and they are valuable when we need help surviving. Life is not always going to be smooth sailing. We all have to work hard from time to time, and if we have developed effective coping skills, we can adjust more easily.

Outer values are learned values that have helped us get to this point in life. They are not to be abandoned; neither are they to be identified with. For example, in a job interview, you may present yourself to your prospective boss as a hardworking individual, yet if hard work is not your core value, you may want to talk about your relevant core values, too. When we talk about our core values, we shine. We become passionate and that passion is what makes us attractive. The hiring manager will interview many self-proclaimed hardworking individuals, but what makes one candidate stand out from another is not their ability to rattle off their outer values, but to share with great passion and joy their inner values.

Ultimately, true and deep satisfaction comes from being and experiencing life as the real you, stripped of everything that is not inherently yours. When you show up in any circumstance as your true, core self, not hiding from your battle wounds and scars, you become magnetic. You will attract those who see the real you and will like you for who you are. When you hide behind your wounds or show them off, you attract those who are attracted to your pain. The choice is yours.

Congruence

Living a life of congruent core values means that you are being true to yourself in all aspects (home, work, friends, etc.) of your life. If justice is a core value, are you being fair to yourself? Are you demanding the same of yourself as you do of others? Most of the warriors I work with do not. They are incredibly hard on themselves and demanding to the point of not being able to meet their own expectations. This is a sure way to guarantee failure and dissatisfaction.

Congruence is not just about the outer world being in alignment with you. It is more about an inner congruence. In other words, are you being true to you? If you are complaining about not being appreciated, and appreciation and recognition are core values to you, then how often and how much do you appreciate and acknowledge yourself? When we fill our spirits up with living our own core values internally, the outer world and their congruence with us do not matter as much.

The emptiness we usually feel is not due to what anyone has or has not done to or for us. The emptiness we feel is due to the derailment that has occurred from us not being true to our own core values. When we continue to feed into a system that does not care about us, we are draining our own natural resources, our own sense of well-being, and eventually we will become physically ill. Our careers are devoid of feeling love or compassion.

By definition, the corporate world exists to make money and to keep its shareholders happy, regardless of what services or products that it provides.

When you pour your heart and soul into a job that you fill purely to make money for someone else and get a little yourself, and it doesn't work out for you, you are left empty, disillusioned, and bitter. Work because you want the money or the currency to spend on what you need and value. Work because you enjoy the work.

If you are working to make the money to buy a lifestyle that you think you want because you never had it, or because you want to be a martyr for your children, then you are working only for the money. If money is your core value, then go ahead with this pursuit. If money is not your core value, then what you have at the end of the day is a series of dissatisfactions. You are bitter and angry because you are not expressing your core values and you are tired for doing the work that does not satisfy or honor who you are.

> **When we continue to feed into a system that does not care about us, we are draining our own natural resources, our own sense of well-being, and eventually we will become physically ill.**

When working in an environment and for people who are incongruent with your core values, you will find yourself drained, because you have been pouring yourself into the wrong vessel.

Perhaps it is time for you to consider changing jobs or careers to find something that aligns more closely with your core values. This might mean that you will need to settle for a lower income. This might mean working alone or drawing attention to your unique abilities and preferences after you have worked so hard to belong to a mainstream group. This might mean that all of the work that you invested in earning all of your degrees and landing your dream job with your dream company is not your dream after all. This might also mean that your children will not be able to do all the things that you had hoped for them. Can you live with that? Can you live with less (money, power, acceptance, and glory) so you can have more (of you) in the end? These are the questions you should be asking yourself when you get that dream job offer.

Most of us live incongruent lives. We may have had congruent moments, but for the most part, our lives are not constructed so that we can express our core values consistently. Living an incongruent life is an opportunity for more outer values to form. In other words, incongruence either forces us to value what the outer world we live in values, or pushes us to develop values for coping. It is how we get to be part of mass consciousness. It is how we become anesthetized and stop thinking about who we are and what we really want. It also helps further develop negative beliefs such as, "That is just the way it is" No one really enjoys their work anyway," or, "I'm doing this for my kids."

Review

Let's look at the story again:

After yet another good performance review, she left his office feeling unappreciated and undervalued. She sat at her desk not understanding why she didn't get the promotion she thought she deserved. She had met all of her goals and achieved them efficiently to his surprise. Yet, he seemed to be grasping for words of praise during her review. She couldn't understand why others were promoted before her. They had not achieved as much and were not as hard working as she was, and yet they were being rewarded far more than she was. She remembered his words, "you need to speak up more in meetings." But the meetings where he wanted her to speak up were for VPs and above. She was only a manager and she did not think it was appropriate to speak up when the higher ups were there, especially if she disagreed with them. Besides, she had to do more fact checking before forming an opinion. It would be disrespectful and shameful if she said something that wasn't true…

The NEW Un-filtered Conversation: I have relied on my own values and strengths to carry me through some of the toughest times and struggles. In the depths of my battles, I forgot that they were my values and strengths. I had assumed that everyone had the same ones, and I overlooked the possibility that my boss's values may be different from mine. I also have to realize that my new culture may embrace different values. I have to ask myself whether I can change or adopt these new values.

It is time again for reflection to apply what you have learned about values. Take a few good deep breaths and start with the exercises below.

Exercise:

1. What are your top three core values? When did you last express them? How often do you live by them?
2. What are your top three outer values? How have you adopted them?
3. What is an outer value that you wish you could let go of?
4. What are some jobs or type of work that would allow you to express most of your core values consistently? What would you have to give up if you were working those jobs?

CHAPTER 5

Big-picture Perspective

Being detached and disconnected enabled her to see what she couldn't see before. She was concerned about this new way she was looking at the world. Now that she had given up trying to fix what seemed to have been broken, what did that mean for her? She felt isolated and removed. Was she just cold and evil? Did she not care about those misfortunate people around her? And what about taking care of her children? Was she supposed to let them do whatever they wanted and not worry about their choices? In some strange way, she felt like there was no point in living. It wasn't that she didn't want to live, there just wasn't a reason to carry on the way she had been and she didn't know how else to be. She felt like she had slid and fallen off the edge of reality into an abyss where she didn't know how to get out.

Self-awareness was the first tool discussed in Chapter 4. Another tool that I highly recommend for anyone who is on the path of living life in a new way is what I call the "big-picture perspective" tool. Once you learn to use self-awareness, the next natural step is to try to take in as much of what is happening as possible. You can do this by focusing on the big picture instead of narrowly gazing at whatever story you are stuck in.

A New Tool

Certain tools are essential in making significant life changes. The ability to see the big-picture perspective is an essential tool that works in tandem with self-observation. Once you can separate yourself from your experience, you are able to truly see the big picture. We are so microscopic in our view of life. This is especially true when things are not as great as we'd like them to be. In moments of despair or anger, we only see what brought us here, and we live and relive the steps and the sequence that we believe led us to the place where we are now. We become attached to our perspective and what we believe to be the truth. The big-picture perspective helps dismantle certain aspects of this so-called reality.

Looking at our situation from the big-picture perspective allows us to see more than our own opinions. In a sense, it disables the ego. We see all the pieces that form the puzzle and realize that we, our problems, and our perspective are just one piece of this puzzle. The big-picture perspective allows us to see how the roles of other people, our own belief systems, our core and outer values, mass consciousness, and our fears have created the reality that we find ourselves locked in.

The big-picture perspective helps us disconnect from the so-called reality. By doing so, it creates a space where there was none. It is similar to taking a deep breath, but it is a mental exercise, so it is like taking a deep breath for your brain. When you realize that you are but a small piece of the puzzle, you are relieved from the extreme sense of responsibility or the perception of impending doom that might have been blocking your view.

When Do I Use the Big-picture Perspective as a Tool?

As with any tool, the more you use it, the more comfortable and natural it becomes. I recommend using it in any and every situation, so that with practice, it becomes second nature. Instead of reacting to your situation, you learn to observe, disconnect, and then act, if you are so inclined. It is the hardest to use in testy situations with your loved ones. They are the ones who are hooked into you and who therefore provide the most challenging situations.

Take the example of having a heated conversation with your teenager about working harder in school. He acts as if he knows everything and you don't. You try to talk to him, put yourself in his shoes, and help him out. After all, you love him and want what's best for him. And it all falls on deaf ears. The big-picture perspective will demonstrate how connected you are to the outcome of his success. The fact that you want something for him makes it impossible to disconnect.

If you could see the big picture of both of your lives and the possible long-term outcomes, you'd realize that there is no need for the heated conversation in which you were so engaged. This does not mean that you shouldn't talk to your son about his performance in school, but how many of us speak from an impartial position? If we speak with the passion that implies that if they don't do well, it is a reflection on us, then we are connected for all the wrong reasons.

The big picture can be just a larger perspective of what is going on, or it can encompass an even bigger picture that includes the past, present and future. You can make it as large as you want. The bigger it is, the greater your sense of calm and ease.

It might be easier to test it out in non-volatile situations. A good place might be at a work meeting where your participation is not essential. You can then focus on observing instead of talking or reacting. Watch the players; observe their motivations, reactions, and how they interact with and affect other people in the room.

After the meeting, think about how you may have acted in a similar situation where your participation was vital. How attached were you to the outcome of the meeting? How attached were you to your point of view? How open were you to the other players? How much does your opinion matter or affect the big picture? These are all questions to ask yourself in your practice of applying the big-picture perspective tool.

Self-awareness is also important here. Observe yourself as you ask yourself these questions. How do you feel? Is your heart rate increasing? Are you feeling anxious? Are you judging yourself for not taking action? Do you feel like you have to save something or someone?

How Do I Use It?

- Observe

First, imagine a short wall between you and the big picture you are looking at. The wall is there to remind you that you are not in the picture, but observing it from outside. From that safe distance, examine the picture objectively. Who is in the picture? What is in the picture? Write your observations and feelings in your journal.

Notice how you are feeling right now. What does all of this observation and note taking do to you? Are you comfortable, agitated, or anxious? Are any fears coming up? Write them down and observe your own reaction to your fears. Notice the sensations in your body. Are your breaths shallow or deep? Is your heart racing or beating normally?

Now take a deep breath and make sure that you are still behind the short wall. Continue to look toward the picture and notice whether the landscape or view is changing. Do you hear any voices? Are you hearing any old tapes, such as your parents or someone telling you this is all a big waste of time? Write it all down in your journal. Try not to judge your experience. Accept whatever you experienced and report it in your journal as an objective journalist would.

- Depersonalize

If you notice feelings of anxiety or stress, try to depersonalize. Remember that you are merely the observer of even yourself in the story. Think of it as not being about you. The point of this exercise is to remove yourself from the story. Any feelings of tension that you notice during this process should be merely acknowledged, and not feared, avoided, or denied. If you are feeling anxious, it is okay. Don't judge yourself for it—this is part of the process. Breathe and allow yourself to feel uncomfortable. If you allow it to be there, it won't last long.

Notice whether you are feeling or acting defensively or trying to rationalize your reaction to your observations. If you are, then at this stage, you could be facing some deeply-rooted belief systems, fears, or other people's belief systems that have been passed on to you, or your own aspects (aspects are pieces of you from your past). We all have past aspects and the richer our lives, the more aspects we have. We have used these aspects to navigate through various stages of our lives. Sometimes, they pop up unexpectedly. For example, you may notice that you are acting like a little child having a tantrum, a young girl hoping to be saved, or being defensive, as you had to be to fight off a rough childhood.

Regardless of what is going on, depersonalize. No matter how deeply affected you think you are, it is not about you.

Depersonalization disengages the ego and now you have a much better chance to see what's happening with clarity.

- Belief Systems

During your practice of noting your experiences with objectively observing and experiencing the big-picture perspective, write down all the belief systems that reveal themselves (we'll cover belief systems in more detail in Chapter 6). Briefly, belief systems are your own beliefs about something, for example, "Good parenting means I have to be more involved in my child's school; if you don't work hard, you won't amount to anything; success means you have to be making $X by the time you are Y years old," and so forth.

You will be surprised at how many belief systems rule your life and your emotions, judgments, and expectations. Making a master list of all of your belief systems is a good idea. It will help you to learn specifically what beliefs are unconsciously prompting you to take certain actions, feel certain feelings, or think certain thoughts. This process is somewhat about identifying the source or the author of the rule book by which you have been abiding, but is primarily about learning what is actually written in the book.

- Disconnect

Disconnection is a result of the practice of truly seeing the big-picture perspective. In other words, you don't have to actively do anything, it just happens. Once you have observed yourself, taken an inventory or your belief systems, and depersonalized, you are disconnected.

Now the drama unfolds like a plot in a movie. You are merely an observer of the movie. You don't feel like you are immersed in the movie as a player, even though you are. From this place, you can make decisions that are for your highest good and that of others. These decisions are not ego-based decisions. They speak to who you truly are.

A counter-intuitive result of disconnecting is its effect on your relationships. You might assume that by being disconnected you are going to be ignored or cast aside. You might initially experience some loneliness, but the relationships that are being cast aside are those that do not honor who you truly are. Disconnecting allows for new, richer, more meaningful relationships to form or deepen. You will start to attract people who notice your wisdom and grace and lose those who want you to play in their drama.

> **You might assume that by being disconnected you are going to be ignored or cast aside. You might initially experience some loneliness, but the relationships that are being cast aside are those that do not honor who you truly are.**

Sometimes, those closest to us, such as our families and dearest friends will begin acting out during this period of disconnecting. They sense that something is different about you and subconsciously they miss the old you. They do things to get your attention and get you back into their drama or the drama you used to share together.

This is extremely challenging, because you are still new to disconnecting and you find yourself being drawn back, sometimes viciously, into the old way of being. You might worry that you are not doing it right or that it just isn't working. Worse yet, you might start questioning the entire process. Perhaps you fear that you are not being a good mother or wife. When you reach this point in the journey, remember to breathe.

Your loved ones don't want to lose you, and they feel like you are vaporizing away. They may not understand that you are not disappearing, but your old personality is. The way you used to show up is disappearing and that is what you wanted. You wanted change, and now it is happening and everyone is freaking out! Just continue to disconnect and allow them to have their drama about it.

Compare this process to what happens when a compulsive overeater or other substance addict begins to heal. It is quite common for the family and friends of someone who is choosing a new, healthier eating style or who is leaving an addiction behind, to offer them food or their drug of choice. These families and friends will often accuse the former addict of changing for the worse, and they may long for the old, addicted personas with whom they are familiar. Their conscious intentions are not usually meant to sabotage the person who has chosen to heal, but rather to maintain the comfortable status quo.

This is a normal human instinct, and you should expect to experience this. It will take time for those you love and who love you to grow comfortable with your true self, but when they do, life will undoubtedly be better for those who accept and embrace you as you truly are.

Compassion

With consistent and frequent practice of using the big-picture perspective tool, at some point you will find yourself confronted with your own understanding of the concept of compassion. Compassion might have meant to feel bad about the injustices of the world. However, after practicing the big-picture perspective method of observation, you will begin to realize that you no longer have an overpowering sense of justice or injustice.

If you are the sensitive kind, you will always feel sorrow over injustices in the world, but you won't go into a tirade about what needs to be done and who needs to be punished. This does not imply being passive and not caring about hunger or war, it means being wise enough and removed enough to realize that "fighting" a war is a war in itself. When we overtly take sides in any situation, we become part of the situation and when we are part of the situation, we cannot help the situation. The situation is stronger than we are, and we are now part of the problem. The only way we can truly help the situation is by staying out of it, so there is at least one less person sucked into the drama. Once you have dismantled the belief system of right vs. wrong, you stop sticking your neck out or feeling sad and eventually drained about something tragic. This is a controversial subject.

I know that when I was younger, I was sure of what was right and what was wrong. Now I realize that when you do that, you are taking away the multidimensionality of the whole situation. How often have we realized that what may have been a "wrong" thing that happened to us (we were really sick), was ultimately good (we missed out on having to go to work only to find out that the important meeting we had planned to attend was cancelled).

When we look at the right vs. wrong story, we are looking at a linear story. Life is not linear. Bad stuff happens and people learn and grow from it. When we are constantly walking around with our magic wands and erasers evaporating or erasing negative experiences for others, we are denying them an opportunity to learn. It is very much like parenting, in that we have to allow our children to learn from their mistakes no matter how hard it is to sit and watch. I like to think of it as allowing and trusting, not passively watching.

I choose to consciously allow and trust that life will work itself out. This does not mean that we sit around and not take action. Action that is taken from true compassion is conscious action, not a reaction stemming from righteousness or anger. Helping someone who asks for your help, if you are truly able to help them, is positive action—not a counter-productive *reaction*.

This may sound callous or even cruel, but you really can't be as effective making sustainable changes in your own life and the lives of others if you are busy taking sides. The new meaning of compassion involves the total acceptance of all that is, even if it seems ugly at first glance. Compassion goes hand-in-hand with honor and respect. How many of us honor and respect a homeless person begging for money on the side of the street? Most of us don't. We want to make it better for them, we wish they weren't there, we

> **Action that is taken from true compassion is conscious action, not a reaction stemming from righteousness or anger.**

think about fixing the system, we wonder about why they don't or can't have a job, and a million other possible scenarios.

Our brain, working in tandem with our ego, can change the meaning of compassion. True compassion is based on the premise that all is well, everyone makes choices based on their circumstances, and more than anything, they want our respect and acceptance of their right to make those choices. No one wants to be fixed, because no one wants to think of themselves as broken. The greatest gift we can give anyone is to accept them for who they are and what they are experiencing, and that is true compassion. This new definition might be disturbing to some. You might find yourself wondering what, if anything, is your purpose? If no one needs you and you don't have to fix anything, then why are you here?

Review

Let's look at the story again:

Being detached and disconnected enabled her to see what she couldn't see before. She was concerned about this new way she was looking at the world. Now that she had given up trying to fix what seemed to have been broken, what did that mean for her? She felt isolated and removed. Was she just cold and evil? Did she not care about those misfortunate people around her? And what about taking care of her children? Was she supposed to let them do whatever they wanted and not worry about their choices? In some strange way, she felt like there was no point in living. It wasn't that she didn't want to live, there just wasn't a reason to carry on the way she had been and she didn't know how else to be. She felt like she had slid and fallen off the edge of reality into an abyss where she didn't know how to get out.

The NEW Un-filtered Conversation: Becoming a new person means discontinuing the person I used to be. The discontinuing comes before the new becoming. I have to die in order to live. Death is scary. What if I actually die?

Take a deep breath. Your buttons may have been pushed. You may not be feeling comfortable after reading this chapter. Take another deep breath and when you feel ready, get your journal, and start working on the following exercises.

Exercise:

1. Practice using the *big-picture perspective* approach in at least three different scenarios in your day. Do this for a month. Keep a journal and write your answers to the

questions that were posed in this chapter (under the subtitle, *How Do I Use It?*).
2. Now that you have practiced using it, what are your observations? What did you learn about yourself? How do you feel?
3. If you are uncomfortable with the ideas that were explored in this chapter, how do you plan to move forward?
4. What do you think about what was written about compassion? How does this definition affect your own experiences of compassion?

CHAPTER 6

Belief Systems

She was wiping the tears off her cheeks and eyes. How could this have happened to her, to them? She had no idea anything was wrong in their marriage. How could he have done this to her? How could she not have seen the signs? She was so smart; she should have seen the signs. She was busy taking care of the kids, her career, making plans for the holidays, organizing their vacations, being a good wife and mom. If there were any signs, she was too tired to have noticed them. So all the hard work, being a good person, marrying the "right" guy, being a good mother, daughter and wife, and this was her reward. How was she going to tell everyone, their friends, her parents, and colleagues? How could she have been so stupid?

The predictability of the lives we create keeps us grounded. Predictability creates the illusion of order and control and slows things down. We believe that creating and maintaining careful order and predictability allows us to control our lives. Order also feeds into the illusion of power. Powerful people lead seemingly well-controlled lives.

Predictability is an important element of classical art. It is aesthetically pleasing to look at symmetrical designs and structures. Beauty is defined and studied to contain certain necessary elements in a certain order or sequence. When we see something that is not pleasing to the eye, we can point to what stands out or doesn't belong. If only it was smaller, bigger, less vibrant, more vibrant, or (fill in the blank). Our attempt to control our surroundings provides satisfaction. However, it is a game that never ends. There is always something to move, remove, add, or improve. It is a state that we strive to achieve, but never quite do.

Belief systems were created to help us make sense of the world. They provide a false sense of reassurance and order. When major life changes confront us, our belief systems are no longer valid and we panic, because nothing makes sense any more. People with similar belief systems hang out together. They share their beliefs with each other and justify them. In fact, many criticize those who have different belief systems, and by doing so, feel more secure about their own. This is when drama, adversity, and negativity are created.

What Are Belief Systems?

Belief systems are the sets of things we believe in. In the case of the woman described at the beginning of this chapter, she believed that if she did all the "right" things in life, everything would go favorably for her. In other words, good things happen to good people. She also believed in being smart and the idea that, "smart people have better control of their lives." Belief systems were created to give meaning to the seemingly senseless nature of life. When you believe in good vs. bad or right vs. wrong then you can motivate yourself to do good or right things in hope of being rewarded a "good" life.

When, as in this case, your belief system is challenged, you are left powerless. Who is this woman if she cannot trust her own intelligence and sense of goodness? Who is she if not a good, hardworking, and smart person? When belief systems are challenged, your whole identity is challenged and that is scary.

The source of our belief systems can be traced back to religion, culture, literature, our own upbringing and mass consciousness in general. Sometimes they tend to justify our actions like, "If you want it done right, do it yourself." Sometimes they motivate us through challenging times, like, "no pain, no gain." Some are conclusions drawn from observing trends like the belief that, "if you earn an Ivy League education, you can land any job you want."

Many times, as in the case of the warriors about whom this book was written, beliefs evolve from parental fears, or fears related to their circumstances. The drive to achieve is born within the fear of failure. The fear motivates the push to make things work out, use the available opportunities, attempt to please parents, or make them proud. Once again, these motivators may not be congruent with our core values and yet somehow in the midst of pushing our way out of what was a difficult situation we forgot who we are.

Belief systems are a creation of duality or opposites. The 3-D world we live in is created from the concept of opposites. We learn by seeing or experiencing the opposite of something. For example, we learned about being good from someone who probably wasn't good to us. We learned to seek wealth because we don't want to be poor. Our belief systems, like good vs. bad or right vs. wrong, have all been created to make sense of things and to control our thoughts and help us make choices. For the most part, they are effective coping skills for adapting to societal norms. It is only when you start questioning the meaning of life that you start unraveling what you believed to be true.

No matter how they developed, the common factor among all belief systems is that they control our thinking and behavior.

Our beliefs hold us in place and generally do not allow for change or growth.

They are in the tenets we cling to, sometimes without conscious awareness. Sometimes our belief systems become visible during a traumatic event, like the woman in the story who suddenly realized that she had believed her intelligence would protect her, only after her husband had left her for another woman and had managed to deceive her, despite how smart she was.

Another example I've observed frequently is the person who is devoutly religious, attends church every Sunday, does well by his or her community and family, and yet a tragic accident takes away a loved one. They tend to question, "Why did this happen?" The underlying assumption is once again that bad things are not supposed to happen to good, devout people. In this case, the person's belief in God and their relationship with God is being questioned, and for a devout believer, that is devastating.

> **Belief systems can also be looked upon as rules that we live by. All is well until the rules don't work anymore. And eventually, they won't.**

Belief systems can also be looked upon as rules that we live by. All is well until the rules don't work anymore. And eventually, they won't. That is when anger sets in, people withdraw from their social connections, and depression takes over. The warriors in this book are the ones who are questioning that anger and depression. They had set out to create a glorious life and will not be content with anything less. After realizing that what used to work for them does not anymore, they are willing to go deep and consciously make the changes that will free them from the cycle of battling opposites. Life then becomes an experience.

The Most Difficult Beliefs to Release

In the case of professional bicultural women, many of their belief systems have helped them get through life and achieve their accomplishments. They may be least likely to entertain the possibility of giving up some of their belief systems. Their lives have been built as a result of their beliefs, or so they wholeheartedly believe. Letting go of their formula for success and a better life is not going to be easy. They are willing to change, but when they realize what needs to change, they resist.

These warriors believe that they have to push hard to get what they want. They live in a world of strife and struggle. This is why they are also referred to as warriors in this book. Unfortunately, these habitual soldiers sometimes forget that the war is over. They continue fighting because their belief is so strong, that it has embedded itself into their every experience. In other words, they don't know how to be anything other than a warrior. The warrior mentality creates and craves conflict as sustenance for its existence. It is essential to note that conflicts aren't necessarily outward battles with others. They may be internal battles, as they usually are.

A strong sense of justice that overrides the joy in most experiences because of an unnatural obsession with achieving fairness is one example of an internal conflict. The internal conflict could be about a need to be liked or accepted that controls our protagonist in every situation. The stronger her belief, the more readily she seems to be looking for its opposite. In other words, she might be searching for injustice, or her senses are finely tuned to recognize and react to signs of injustice, if being fair is one of her belief systems. It is almost as if her reason for living is to prove and live out her belief systems, and to battle anything that represents the opposite of what she believes in.

Regardless of what the most difficult or controlling belief system is, its effects control every aspect of her life. It is as though her beliefs are the only lens through which she is capable of viewing and experiencing her life. Throwing away this filter means she won't be able to view life as she is accustomed to living it. This elicits in her the fear of blindness. Once she trusts that she is not blind and adjusts her eyes to this new way of seeing, she is likely to find a new and wonderful world that was always in front of her, just beyond the artificial lens she had created with her belief system.

Letting go of old belief systems is not easy, and it guarantees change of the deepest kind. Yet even though most people say they want change, most may not be ready for real change. They may want a better life, more money, or a better relationship, but change that is out of their control and unpredictable or unimaginable is not a comforting kind of change, no matter what its potential benefits. What's worse is the trauma of the event that causes this change. When you cling tenaciously to an old belief system, it sometimes takes a big jolt of something unpleasant like a divorce, loss of a job, or a health crisis to release it. If you can convince yourself to view your crisis as the *solution* to your problem, the transition becomes much more graceful and its lessons more profound.

What to Expect When You Change Your Belief Systems

When you change your belief systems, everything else in your life changes accordingly. For example, imagine not believing in good vs. bad. If you don't believe that anything is good or bad, you can't engage in the same battles or games. Changing your belief systems may also mean that you cannot always keep the same company, because their games and battles grow boring or silly to you. You no longer rush into secondary and tertiary beliefs that are offshoots of the original one, and your belief in achieving justice or fairness will disappear. You don't act from reflex. Rather you think more consciously, and you become more thoughtful and deliberate in your actions. Your life will change profoundly for the better.

This level of change is unfamiliar and frightening. Where belief systems defined rigid rules, there is now open space with room to think and feel freely. It feels like you are all alone in a strange landscape, one you couldn't have even imagined under your old belief system. To make matters worse, you are alone, because not many people have travelled this road. The people you used to hang out with are no longer your companions, and it feels extremely lonely.

Even though you chose and embraced this change, you now question whether you have made the right decision. This is when it is important to remember that change means different, not "better" as defined by your old understanding of "good." When you choose change, you simultaneously let go of how it shows up and what that means. Change is difficult only because it is unpredictable and we adult humans have a difficult time handling uncertainty. We gravitate toward the familiar as a moth to a flame. Yet change can become familiar and comfortable if we eagerly embrace it and patiently watch and wait to discover its benefits over time.

Addictions

Chaos is the opposite of predictability. In chaos, there is no order, and our belief systems don't work there. We are left powerless. Change makes things unpredictable. Change brings us closer to chaos and farther away from order. Change uproots us, and what was solid now becomes fluid and murky.

We crave the stability and safety of order and predictability. In the midst of chaos and change we cling to what we think will make us feel safe: food, sex, work, family drama, staying busy, spending money, saving money, or whatever habits previously gave us comfort. This is when addictions or obsessions take over. Addictions numb us from feeling the fear of losing control. Compulsive behavior shields us from having to face other matters. It filters out the chaos that we fear—the chaos that, if faced directly—would allow us to grow and experience our lives to the fullest.

When we obsessively do something, think something, or say something, we are fighting the fear of losing control. The same applies to the obsessive exercise addict who has to work out for hours every day to maintain a certain look, and who at times deceives herself that she is doing it for health reasons. It becomes a compulsion, perhaps to hold onto a youth that is slipping by. The same can be said with the workaholic who stays late at work every night, works from home, and on weekends and holidays. At times, she even hates her job, yet she can't seem to get enough of it. It is an addiction. It is an obsession that keeps her busy, so that she will not have to think about the possibility of giving it up. Who would she be without it? Her addiction defines her and offers her a false sense of self.

Review

Now, let's read the story again:

She was wiping the tears off her cheeks and eyes. How could this have happened to her, to them? She had no idea anything was wrong in their marriage. How could he have done this to her? How could she not have seen the signs? She was so smart; she should have seen the signs. She was busy taking care of the kids, her career, making plans for the holidays, organizing their vacations, being a good wife and mom. If there were any signs, she was too tired to have noticed them. So all the hard work, being a good person, marrying the "right" guy, being a good mother, daughter and wife, and this was her reward. How was she going to tell everyone, their friends, her parents and colleagues? How could she have been so stupid?

The NEW Un-filtered Conversation: What if I was so driven by my ego-driven thoughts and actions that the only thing that could have stopped me was a hard fall? What better way to fall than through a good jolt of betrayal? When I look at what happened this way, it almost feels empowering. Something had to stop me. Unfortunately, I had to be stopped because I could not stop myself.

Exercise:

1. What are your top three belief systems?
2. How have your belief systems served you?
3. What is one belief system you'd like to let go of? How will you do it and who will support you?
4. What are some of your obsessions, issues you like to control, or addictions?

CHAPTER 7

Obstacles

I really want to start my own business; I know I would do well. I have all these ideas and when I think about my dream business, I get so excited and happy. I haven't been this excited since I was in college. But in the beginning, I won't make the kind of money I am making now. And what if it isn't successful? I can't make less money. I have a mortgage and two kids in private school. I love my house and the town I live in, we go on great vacations around the world, and I wouldn't be able to live the same lifestyle if I left my job right now. I guess I have to tough it out and bite the bullet for the next ten years. It's just the way it is. Besides, once I get that next promotion, then I can do anything I want.

Obstacles to achieving self-mastery and ultimately a peaceful and fulfilling existence are internal. Internal obstacles include fears, old thinking patterns, belief systems, past negative experiences, doubt, personal aspects, and lack of self-confidence. I previously described how belief systems define our experiences in life and past negative experiences are similar to belief systems. At times, past negative experiences even lead us to form self-defeating belief systems or feed into old belief systems that no longer serve us.

Let's imagine that your trust has been betrayed. You thought you had married a certain someone and had made certain assumptions about them and they let you down. You, as an educated, high-achieving, professional bicultural woman think you are/were smart and yet this still happened to you. How would you feel about entering another relationship? Do you trust yourself when it comes to relationships? Do you start doubting everyone? Have you replaced one belief system (I am a smart woman) with another (men are all jerks)? And can you see how self-defeating this pattern is?

Another major obstacle in the path of self-mastery is not dealing with old transitions. As mentioned in earlier chapters, there was a change (moving to a new culture) that led to the bicultural piece in the lives of the warriors of this book. How you dealt or did not deal with that change remains with you until you address the feelings (suppressed or not), and consciously free whatever needs to be released. Without consciously choosing to let go, you cannot truly move forward.

Fears

For the professional bicultural woman described at the beginning of this chapter, her fear involves the dread of losing an established lifestyle. The fears of most professional bicultural women include: loss of a lifestyle, personal failure, not moving up within the ranks at a certain rate, not being accepted, not fitting in, not being loved, being alone, being poor, struggling like her parents did, being controlled, being cornered or stuck, being stupid, not doing enough, and more. All of these fears can be boiled down to two main ones: the fear of losing an identity and the fear of change, which leads to the loss of an identity.

The two primary fears are related, because once you release your grip on your so-called identity, change begins to happen. And because of all the unknowns, change is not readily embraced until status quo becomes so unbearable that change is inevitable. In other words, you have to be willing to let go of who you were to embrace who you want to be.

This is critical for professional, bicultural women, because they have worked extremely hard to achieve a certain degree of predictability in their lives. They have worked diligently to earn the level of education that will, in turn, secure the high- level job that was supposed to guarantee a better and easier life than the one their parents had. Therefore, they will tolerate a high level of dissatisfaction in their work and relationships, and they will tolerate a lack of fun, joy, or peace to avoid disrupting what they have worked so hard to achieve. The idea that they may have to forfeit what they are so invested in is unfathomable. That is why they usually hit rock bottom before they are willing to change.

> **They suddenly realize that something significant must change. Then the work and the journey of self-mastery begins.**

The rocks that these women tend to hit include divorce (serious marital problems), loss of a job (being demoted, laid off or fired), a devastating health diagnosis, or loss of a parent or loved one. In the state of mind where they feel like they are no longer who they used to be (such as becoming a single mother, unemployed, unhealthy, or an orphan), something happens to them—something out of their control—and after a cooling off period, they suddenly realize that something significant must change. Then the work and the journey of self-mastery begins.

Aspects

Another type of inner obstacle is related to aspects. Aspects are versions of ourselves that were created during various stages of life. We all have certain aspects like the *little child* aspect, the *judge*, the *victim*, and so forth. These aspects were created by us to endure a certain phase or experience in life without breaking emotionally. For example, the bicultural woman created a hard-working aspect to get through school in a new culture. She probably also created a responsible aspect to help with her family, a tough aspect to deal with all the adversity, and so on.

Aspects become obstacles either when they assume control, or when you allow them to take control of your "now" experience. This again is closely tied to belief systems. For example, if you have invested all of your time and energy into your job and yet have been mistreated by management, and you know that it is time to leave, your responsible aspect may attempt to take over. You may then find yourself still working extremely hard to the point of ignoring your future or potential job(s) because of this out-of-control responsible aspect. When aspects go rogue, they undermine the "now" experience. You may become overly obsessive, and even a martyr, to a job that you hate and have chosen to leave. On the surface, it makes no sense, until you realize that you have become a slave to your aspects and belief systems.

The only way to understand what is really happening is to choose awareness. When you become the observer of yourself and are aware of what is going on, you can consciously choose to retire your unnecessary aspects. You can choose to let go of martyrdom, being a good soldier, being a good little girl, or whatever your interfering aspects may be. You may also need to consciously identify and release a stuck belief system, like the one that says being irresponsible is bad. You must release aspects and belief systems to give yourself the freedom to experience life in a new way. It is challenging work to be sure, but it comes with a huge payoff in true joy and freedom to be who you want to be.

Doubt/Lack of Trust

At some point during the busting of old belief systems and aspects, you might find yourself wondering, or perhaps even being certain of, the fact that you may have gone crazy! This is all natural. When you let go of the glue that held your reality together, nothing makes sense anymore. The educated, accomplished, successful, smart person suddenly feels completely foreign in her own life. Her friends or family may demand answers for the changes in behavior. They may wonder if she is depressed, having a crisis, hanging out with the wrong crowd, or assume some other nefarious cause is at work. They may even try an intervention.

When doubt seeps in, you'll start to believe that perhaps your mother is right—you are going a little crazy. Perhaps you've gone too far. Perhaps you could take some pills and be done with your depression, fix your head, and your wayward thinking. But relax. This is all part of the process. In fact, you are probably not far along your journey if you do *not* have any doubts. The key is to recognize your doubts and then free them, just as you have released your old belief systems that no longer serve you. Conscious breathing is very helpful during this entire process.

We connect with others through our beliefs and the actions that follow those beliefs. When we let go of the beliefs, the aspects whose existence depends on our acting out those beliefs start getting annoyed. When you let go of those aspects, then there is an emptiness that used to be occupied with all of the beliefs and aspects, and with the people you used to interact with who shared the beliefs with you. This is when doubt sets in. After all, you chose to go on this path because you were depressed and angry, yet now you are depressed, angry, and alone! You assume that something is wrong.

One way to diffuse doubt is through self-trust. When you trust yourself implicitly, knowing that you couldn't do any wrong, because nothing is wrong, then doubt goes away. It is crucial to remember that what I am talking about here is self-trust, not trust in something outside yourself. Trust is an elusive concept. We have all been let down by those we have trusted at some point in our lives. We have been let down through events that made us mistrustful of our own safety from poverty, health, relationships, or other feared states of being and events. All of these experiences have taken trust out of our lives. We may even find it difficult to trust ourselves because we think that we have done some bad things, or made some wrong decisions. If that is the case, then this is a good time to re-visit those events or decisions. Once you start looking at your decisions through the wise eyes of someone who is open and willing to change, you might see them in a different light. This sub-process will help deepen your self-trust, which will further facilitate your journey.

Self-Confidence or Not?

The more you trust yourself, the more confident you become. The confidence and trust don't come from a mental or logical analysis. For example, imagine someone who has had a very difficult life through difficult relationships. She may have been born into a family who wasn't affectionate or caring, she may have ended up in a marriage that wasn't caring or supportive, or she may have found herself working in jobs where she repeatedly attracted difficult situations where she was wrongly accused of things she didn't do. This person seemingly has no reason to trust herself. She may believe that she just has poor judgment and continue making the same mistakes or attracting the same negative situations or people. That's the logical or intellectual way of viewing her life.

Another way of looking at her situation may be that there are certain patterns that she continues to repeat habitually. The first assumption should become that she is choosing these patterns on an unconscious level. To be a conscious creator, we need to recognize that which has been unconscious and mindfully bring it into the realm of our awareness.

So, what does her pattern of choosing unreliable, unloving, and unsupportive relationships and circumstances offer her? What does she get out of it? Who would she be without these patterns? These are the questions she needs to ask herself and be able to honestly and openly answer them in a safe space. These questions are tantamount to peeling the layers of an onion. There are multiple layers that vary from each other in appearance and complexity, so the layer you reveal today may bring an answer that is substantially different from the answer you find three months from now, and so on.

> **To be a conscious creator, we need to recognize that which has been unconscious and mindfully bring it into the realm of our awareness.**

Once our protagonist has discovered the lesson of her creations without judgment, she can then release them. Confidence is all about truly knowing that you created the circumstances of your life, and you can release what does not work anymore. The first step though, is about acceptance of what is and your role in creating it. Then you can consciously choose to let go and choose instead to live the life you truly desire.

As simple as this sounds, it is not easy. If you have always lived a certain pattern, breaking it is especially difficult. You don't have the confidence or the knowingness to believe that you will survive. Your entire life may have been built on these patterns, and as negative as they may have been, you are comfortable with them, because that is all you have known. You may believe that you cannot invest your trust in something that you have not experienced or known. Trust is to be placed in yourself and no one or nothing else. Now you will need to learn to tap into your inner self and find a way to trust that you know how to take care of yourself no matter what happens. This takes practice.

Review

Let's revisit the story: *I really want to start my own business. I know I would do well. I have all these ideas, and when I think about my dream business, I get so excited and happy. I haven't been this excited since I was in college. But in the beginning, I won't make the kind of money I am making now. And what if it isn't successful? I can't afford to make less money. I have a mortgage and two kids in private school. I love my house and the town I live in, we go on great vacations around the world, and I wouldn't be able to live the same lifestyle if I left my job right now. I guess I have to tough it out and bite the bullet for the next ten years. It's just the way it is. Besides, once I get that next promotion, then I can do anything I want.*

The Un-filtered Conversation: *Even though, I complain about my situation, I am not ready to make a real change. I don't feel comfortable giving up all that I have worked hard to achieve. I like moving up in the organization and having more responsibilities. These achievements make me feel important and powerful.*

Exercise:

Remember to breathe deeply and practice trusting yourself and your real feelings as you write in your journal. You are safe, so simply observe and evaluate without judging yourself.

1. What are your top three obstacles to changing your life?
2. How have you been looking at and handling these obstacles?

4. What are the underlying patterns of these obstacles?
5. How would your life be different if you didn't have these obstacles to face?

CHAPTER 8

Choice

She stood in front of the mirror and dropped the towel to the floor. Her middle-aged body looked older than 47. Her face was sallow and sagging. Her flabby stomach and mid-section repulsed her. How had she let herself go? She remembered a time when she was thin and beautiful. She had worn fashionable clothes and her hair was perfect. Now she doesn't even want to go to the mall. What would be the point? How could she accept the fact that she was two sizes bigger than what she used to be? How embarrassing. She felt ashamed...

Conscious choice is how we create our lives after we let go of all that does not serve us anymore. Conscious choice depends on responsibility. Once we accept that we have co-created the life that we are living, we can attend to the business of changing it. However, in order to be able to consciously choose, we have to first accept and love what we have already chosen. In other words, we need to take responsibility for all of our creations. Taking responsibility or ownership has to come without rational analysis or justification. For example, if you are currently in a dysfunctional relationship, you can't justify it by saying that you are in this situation because your parents were in a dysfunctional relationship, you grew up not knowing any better, and therefore, you accept your current relationship based on that.

What you may have chosen unconsciously is still a very real choice. Ownership has to do with loving your current relationship and all that it has taught you. Within every so-called bad situation, there is always a gift. We often learn from the most challenging people and situations in our lives. We learn how not to be, or how to be, we realize that what we may have labeled as a negative experience, once removed, may have been the best thing that happened. So, what are the gifts you have given yourself?

Acceptance

I spoke about acceptance in Chapter 5 under the heading of compassion. Here, I'd like to discuss self-acceptance. We often find it easier to accept others than we do ourselves. However, to move forward and create the life that we want, we first have to truly accept the life that we have already created. We have to accept the shape we are in right now, not the shape we anticipate we will be in after we lose those unwanted 10 pounds, after we diet, hit the gym, and work on our abs.

Acceptance is the platform on which we create our future. If our platform is shaky, we cannot build a sturdy structure, and no one will believe our creations to be of value, including us. It makes the journey of spiritual awakening and self-mastery a joke. Can we accept our age, the person we are married to, relationships, body, financial status, home, job, or other circumstances and choices? Perhaps acceptance is a neutral word and does not resonate with you. Perhaps the question to ask is: Can you choose to love your age, the person you are married to, relationships, body, financial status, home, job, and

> **Acceptance is the platform on which we create our future. If our platform is shaky, we cannot build a sturdy structure.**

other choices that have brought you to where you are today? This is when it gets to be difficult.

This is especially challenging because of common belief systems. For example, if you are overweight, you are constantly judging yourself, and society reinforces your self-criticism. You turn on the television and see all the skinny, beautiful people, all the weight loss products, and the programs that you are expected to buy to conform to an unrealistic standard. You try on your old jeans and they don't fit, your nose could be smaller, your skin could be more perfect, and so on. How can you love yourself with all of these expectations from yourself and from society? The truth is that you can't love yourself if you choose to continue to buy into the hype.

You first have to detach from the outer belief systems, the outer world, and its messages. Once you have quieted that voice, you need to stop listening to your own. You will probably start rationalizing by telling yourself *"Well, I am really a nice person, so it doesn't matter that I'm overweight" or fill in the blanks for whatever seems to counter the false beliefs.* Stop rationalizing, because that is a scapegoat. Try connecting to the feeling of love in your heart. Imagine all the people you deeply love and from that place, connect back to yourself. Can you love yourself unconditionally right now, exactly the way you are?

Self-acceptance and self-love do not imply that we are happy with status quo and won't do anything to change. It means that we are so in love with ourselves that we continue to create, express, and experience. A loving creator does not have to destroy her old creation in order to create a new one. Loving her original creation, she then moves on to create something else or to transform what she has already created. The key is to love, honor, and accept even that which may seem unlovable.

Stop the Fighting

Acceptance is about peace. When we refuse to accept something, we are at war with it. We are either trying to change it, avoiding it, denying it, hating it, analyzing it, or crying about it. It all boils down to fighting a war in which we are the ones to lose. Whether you are fighting your war publicly or privately, the outcome is sure; you are going to find yourself even more stuck than before. Acceptance is about peace and the release of the need to fight.

If you find this difficult to believe, consider our national war on drugs. It is an abysmal failure, by any measure. I'm not suggesting that we encourage drug abuse; rather I am suggesting that by focusing on the fight, we manifest what we focus on. We might well do better to focus on the joys of conscious living than fighting medicated and unconscious living.

Most of the time, we are not even aware of the wars we are fighting. They don't seem like wars. It is how we have lived our lives and how others live theirs. In other words, "if you are not happy about something, just go ahead and change it and then you will be happy." This type of thinking is what gets us stuck every time. The belief that happiness is something that can be achieved through obtaining or achieving something else, is a myth that creates most of the resistance and battles in our lives.

Happiness is not about achieving anything. Happiness is not experienced through outer events. If it were so, then it would feed into the meaninglessness and randomness of life, which is extremely disempowering.

When we truly accept the current state of our creations, when we love what we have created, then we can freely create what we love.

It is also about accepting our creatorship. In other words, in order to feel empowered, you have to first accept responsibility for what you have already created. You have to accept the fact that there are no random events and mishaps. Everything that has happened has happened in a perfect sequence to bring you to this perfect moment, the now moment.

True acceptance brings true peace. True peace is liberating, safe, warm, welcoming, nurturing, loving, and beautiful. From this place you can choose anything you want.

The Nature of Reality

The 3-D reality we live in is based in duality. Everything has an opposite, and we create our reality based on the battles between opposites. It also works in terms of force. We push and force things to happen. We expend a certain amount of energy. However, for every push or force, there is a counter force. That is the reason why fighting doesn't work.

The more we fight, the more we get accustomed to the experience of fighting, so much so that we learn to find comfort in fighting. It becomes a way of life, and it is how we experience being alive. The tension that is created through duality is how most humans experience life on this planet. Add to this natural tension the inherent nature of a difficult life with its many challenges, and you have the experience of a true warrior who does not know how to exist outside of battle. Ironically, true warriors like the ones described in this book are the ones who are ready for change, primarily because they are the ones who are tired of the fighting.

If your battles are easy and you are winning, there is no reason to change, because there is no reason to dislike the life you are living.

You don't question life or seek the spiritual path. A certain amount of difficulty is a requirement to create the curiosity that will motivate you to question the way you have been living. When you realize that difficulty is a prerequisite, then you stop fighting it. You stop blaming it and wallowing in it. You start accepting it, and that is when flow begins.

How and Why We Don't Choose

We don't choose, because we can't choose. We can't choose because we are busy fighting or resisting. Conscious choice happens when you are aware and making deliberate choices. Warriors whose minds are engaged in battle respond unconsciously and make instinctive choices, rather than thinking them through. When we accept responsibility for all of our creations and accept all that is, then and only then can we begin to consciously choose.

We don't choose, because we are afraid of choosing the wrong things. At this point in the journey, we know we are responsible for our choices, so we are overly cautious about making the wrong choices. In a sense, we are gun-shy. We don't trust ourselves and our ability to make the right choices. Therefore, we don't choose. This can be dangerous, because it feeds into the lethargic feel of this part of the journey.

That's why it is so important to not only accept your creations, but to love them as well. Our choices, conscious or not, are a reflection of what we have needed to bring us to this point. When we truly understand this, we can love the life we have created, not just the good parts, but the whole thing. This love can then help build self-trust. Self-trust then helps us to develop the habit of making conscious choices.

Review

Let's revisit the story: *She stood in front of the mirror and dropped the towel to the floor. Her middle-aged body looked older than 47. Her face was sallow and sagging. Her flabby stomach and midsection repulsed her. How had she let herself go? She remembered a time when she was thin and beautiful. She had worn fashionable clothes and her hair was perfect. Now she doesn't even want to go to the mall. What would be the point? How could she accept the fact that she was two sizes bigger than what she used to be? How embarrassing. She felt ashamed...*

The Un-filtered Conversation: *I am not 25 anymore. I don't look 25 anymore and I certainly don't feel it either. I am an older woman with a lot of living behind me and a lot more ahead of me. I do want to feel more healthy and fit, but if working out and eating healthy does not change the shape of my body, I will honor it. In fact, I honor it the way it is right now. I am tired of beating myself up.*

Exercise:

Approach this with an attitude of acceptance...

1. If the idea of loving yourself regardless of your current circumstances seems difficult, imagine that you just adopted an abused and sickly dog from the pound. Everyone around you might say or think that you are crazy for doing such a thing and they might disapprove of your choice of pet. The dog might be a pain to take care of and she might chew up your furniture and relieve herself on your rug. Can you still love her? Can you accept that you are the only one who does? Can you see the potential in

that dog? Now apply the same thinking to yourself. Can you be the only one who loves you? Write your thoughts down.
2. What don't you love about yourself or your life? What if you did love those things? What would your life be like if you loved it all?
3. Think of a mistake that you think you have made. Now, reframe it. Think of it as a choice you made. Write down a list of the gifts that this mistake/choice brought to your life.
4. Have you ever felt stuck? Describe the feeling of being stuck and now reframe it. What if you got yourself stuck, so that you would stay put? What is the gift at this moment of staying put?

CHAPTER 9

In It, But Not of It

Her teenage son slammed the door extra hard as he left, trying to make a point. He hadn't gotten his way and he was angry. She sat down wondering why she wasn't pleased with herself. She had said, "No," to his outrageous demands, she had said, "No more," to the sense of entitlement that teenagers like him have, and she had walked away from the drama that he liked to create. Yet, there was no satisfaction in her heart. She was torn. Was she being a bad mother? Was she too strict and unreasonable? Had she done something to lead them to this point? She sat down with all the questions spinning in her head, feeling devastated, guilt-ridden, and confused.

She felt out of touch with her children. She felt out of touch with the idea of being a mother. She couldn't talk about these things with other friends who were mothers. What would they think of her? Had she gone mad? Had she lost touch with reality?

All she wanted to do was to putter outside in the garden. She would rather pull out weeds in the flower beds than do the dishes. In fact, she despised doing chores that were not fun or creative. She wanted to be out in the sun with the birds and the bugs. This was her bliss.

Mass consciousness and the 3-D world do not support true empowerment. Self-actualized beings who have achieved self-mastery do not feed into belief systems that hold up the world. Therefore, if you have chosen this path, you will feel resistance and even attacks sometimes from the people closest to you.

Complicating this further is the fact that you are new to all of this. As during any transition, you will experience the various phases of change in turn (ending, empty zone, and the new beginning)[2]. Coming to terms with the ending of the way you used to be is important, if not necessary, for your successful journey into the new you. And the middle phase where nothing seems to be happening is always challenging.

During this middle phase, you are not quite the new you and you are still tied to who you were, even though you are not operating in that old way now. You seem to be in a no man's land. The duration of stay in each of these phases is different for everyone, and it is not a linear process. It seems to have multiple layers. Just when you think that you are done with one ending, gone through the empty zone, and beginning a new phase, you find that something else needs to die. You may feel as though you take two steps forward and one step back, but keep in mind that this is still forward progress.

It is precisely during the recognition of your grand transition that you begin to wonder about everyone else in your life. There is a sadness that takes over when you realize that the ones you love dearly may never understand what you are going through and why you are going through it. In the end however, you will find great strength through the loneliness because you will find you—all of you. You will find all the pieces of you that you thought you had lost, and some that you never knew you had. You will emerge fully integrated and whole, and in that wholesomeness, you will not need the company of others who do not understand you.

Once you emerge into your new beginning, and start getting busy again, becoming more comfortable with the new you, you will miss the in-between phase where you were alone and had time and space to emerge from your cocoon. You will miss the cocoon and the peaceful silence that the incubating period offers. This is one example of how a seemingly "bad" situation when looked at from the *big-picture perspective* may not seem "bad" at all.

To Eject or Not

At times, it seems like the only way to be able to live a spiritual life is to leave everything behind. At least that's the way the spiritual leaders of the past have done it. Rest assured, however, that depriving oneself of material goods, food, pleasure, and even the love of our dear ones is not the way of the new spiritual masters.[3] The new spiritual mastery has to do with integrating our human and divine selves. It is about reconciling our human selves with our souls.

I have been asked by the warriors who have inspired this book whether they can go on pursuing and developing their careers while achieving self-mastery on the spiritual path. The question can only be answered by the individual who understands the demands of their career and whether they can meet those demands while remaining true to themselves. Total honesty is the prerequisite in determining whether you need to make a big change like leaving your job. Be honest with yourself when you examine your values, priorities, and desires before making any decisions. Be honest when you evaluate the obstacles, such as fears and belief systems.

Go through the exercises in this book and work with a spiritual coach or facilitator in stretching yourself. When you are clear, you can then make a decision. This will be the first among many decisions that you will use as stakes along the road to real self-discovery.

Expect Lots of Alone Time

The steps below describe what happens when you are going through a major change.

Something triggers the need to change, then you:
1. Earnestly decide to make a change
2. Learn about what it takes to change and what it is exactly that needs to change
3. End the way you did something or a quality or habit about yourself
4. Practice the new way of being or doing
5. Fall off the wagon
6. Don't get the results you had hoped for
7. Lose some relationships either because you don't relate to certain people anymore or find yourself questioning certain relationships
8. Feel lonely and/or alone
9. Recognize that you have changed indeed
10. And finally, new relationships or new-old relationships or new opportunities show up

Steps 5 through 10 cycle repeatedly, and the duration depends on how major the change is. The in-between place is somewhere between steps 6 through 10. There are no remedies, quick fixes, or words of consolation when someone is going through these steps. It is a lonely and introspective time.

Time well spent in these steps can determine the sustainability and success of the transition. This is because real change takes time.

If you rush the time between steps 6 through 10, you are bound to go back to the way you used to be and repeat the whole process. That is what happens to people who jump from one relationship to another marrying or dating a slightly different version of the same person all over again, or take a different job, only to find out they have created the same scenario with their co-workers or boss, just in a different organization.

Living in the world, but not being of it is just what it says. It can be a lonely place at times. Without all the drama, belief systems, rules, aspects, fears, and battles, we are left with little that we are familiar with. In fact, when you choose to make real change, you will find yourself withdrawing from groups and friends you used to associate with and who you no longer relate to. You will shy away from gossip and drama. What is important to most people seems unimportant to you. You are now looking at the big picture and your perspective is different from that held by most others.

In addition, you will become hypersensitive. Every negative or gossip-ridden story will actually make you feel sick and hurt. This is another reason you'd rather be alone than take a chance and be hurt or dragged through some negativity that you don't care about. What interests you are the bigger, deeper things in life, such as what is happening with the world, the environment, religion, and other global concerns You couldn't care less about how Patty's date went last night or how Joanne's Super Bowl party turned out. People's life stories bore you unless they are willing to go deep enough, change and share their experiences with you.

You might be drawn to nature. Going for walks and enjoying nature, birds, and flowers may be suited better to your temperament than hanging out with your friends. You may find yourself drawn to babies or animals. The simple life that has been untouched by humans seems more desirable to you now.

Your reading tastes may also change. You may be seeking self-help or spiritual books in place of a novel. This too, will not last. In fact, you may have a stack of books from different genres by your bed. At times, it might seem like you don't know what to expect, your moods and tastes seem to change constantly. You are unpredictable even to yourself.

Explorer

You become an explorer in your own life. Like a world traveler, you'll find yourself exploring all aspects of what has been and still is. You start examining things with fresh eyes, curious as to what has been motivating you all along. You'll move through events unscathed, like a tourist attending a festival in a foreign land. You have a deeper understanding of the concept of detachment. You aren't burdened by what appears to be happening.

This is the gift of seeing the *big-picture perspective* all the time. Your friends and family may not be supportive of the explorer in you, because you may seem cold, detached, boring, and unavailable. You may not be participating in conversations that seem small and petty. In other words, you have changed and they do not like the new you, mainly because it implies that you find them boring or uninteresting. They may question the new you, ask you if you are depressed, accuse your new friends or interests of turning you against your family, and wonder why you are so quiet.

You don't have a need to share your journey with those you know would not understand or approve. You don't want to judge them and certainly don't need them to judge you. In fact, you may not even be sure that you are on the right path. You just know that what was, no longer makes sense. There is an urgency to change and you have no desire to convince anyone else to do the same. You are not an evangelist, just an explorer.

New/Old Connections and Interests

You may start to pull back from some friendships because you'll have little in common with them. In turn, other older friendships may feel more comfortable. You may reconnect with an old high school friend, or a cousin you grew up with and find the new/old connection refreshing and comfortable. Perhaps your old friend or cousin knew the old you and now you have a better understanding of the old you too. Now you have a new platform to build your relationship on.

Old understandings may change. For example, if you thought a parent was a certain way and you blamed them for certain events, you may now see the old situation in a new light. With a different perspective, you may now have closure, healing, and release of an old, painful memory. This will change your relationship with the parent. You may reach out to them, and forgive them.

Creativity becomes an important outlet. You may re-visit old hobbies and/or interests. Chores and daily activities may seem pointless, and you might find yourself spending hours painting, writing, or creating. You might even start a new hobby to learn something you've always wanted to try. These creative activities may be the most joyful and fulfilling part of your life.

Included in the newly blossoming creativity, is the joy you will find in the simple activities of everyday life. The only way you can get yourself to do the menial jobs of the day is to break it down into small steps and slow down enough to enjoy them. This is a result of a certain kind of intolerance for anything harsh or negative. Pushing yourself to do five loads of laundry is exactly that, unless you can see the beauty and joy in taking care of yourself by cleaning your clothes.

Your intuitive knowledge grows exponentially. You know things without knowing how you know them. You know instinctively when the phone is going to ring and who is on the line. You may wish for something, the doorbell will ring, and what you wished for will have arrived for you inexplicably. These types of activities will become so much more frequent that you will no longer see them as being out of the norm. Problems will be solved miraculously or answers will come to you in dreams. Life becomes smoother and easier.

All of these manifestations of your new internal life will further distance you from others who are not going through it. That is why it is so important to have a friend who you can share your inner most experiences with. If that is not feasible in your life, then it is crucial to find a spiritual coach or facilitator who you trust to work with. It will feel like the only person you can be open with is someone who has walked in your shoes.

[2] Bridges, William: *The Way of Transition, Embracing Life's Most Difficult Moments.* De Capo Press, 2001.

[3] Adamus Saint-Germain: *Masters in the New Energy.* Crimson Circle Press, 2007.

Review

Let's revisit the story: *Her teenage son slammed the door extra hard as he left, trying to make a point. He hadn't gotten his way and he was angry. She sat down wondering why she wasn't pleased with herself. She had said, "No," to his outrageous demands, she had said, "No more," to the sense of entitlement that teenagers like him have, and she had walked away from the drama that he liked to create. Yet, there was no satisfaction in her heart. She was torn. Was she being a bad mother? Was she too strict and unreasonable? Had she done something to lead them to this point? She sat down with all the questions spinning in her head, feeling devastated, guilt-ridden, and confused.*

She felt out of touch with her children. She felt out of touch with the idea of being a mother. She couldn't talk about these things with other friends who were mothers. What would they think of her? Had she gone mad? Had she lost touch with reality?

All she wanted to do was to putter outside in the garden. She would rather pull out weeds in the flower beds than do the dishes. In fact, she despised doing chores that were not fun or creative. She wanted to be out in the sun with the birds and the bugs. This was her bliss.

The NEW Un-filtered Conversation: *What happens when you stop being the way you used to be? I am not sure I know the answer to that. I can't care about others anymore. I feel selfish and uncaring. I can't care about what I used to care about anymore. I see everyone differently now. I am not depressed, just awake. Everyone is playing a game and when you stop playing yours, they still expect you to continue. They'll do anything to get you back in their story. No more…*

Exercise:

1. Think about your life from the beginning. Have you been drawn to groups or organizations? Has this changed with time? What do you think changed it?
2. Think about your friends from the beginning. Have your friends changed with time? What changed your choice of friends? Who would you rather spend time with? If you can't think of anyone, think of the qualities of the person you'd like to have as a friend.
3. What are your creative outlets? Have you had creative hobbies in the past? How have they changed?
4. Describe a perfectly satisfying day. What are you doing? Who are you with? What does it feel like?

CHAPTER 10

Putting It All Together

Nothing had really changed in her outer world. She still had the same issues with her family, her job, her friends, etc. However, she felt different inside. She didn't feel like any of her issues were real. There was this other dimension in which she seemed to go into where nothing really mattered because nothing seemed real. She was afraid of losing her intensity. After all, she loved the highs in her life even though, she hated the lows. She couldn't imagine life without intense joy. But it wasn't about joy or sadness anymore. It was about feeling complete. She was complete and as such, didn't need anything or anyone else to fill her up. She felt like she had not just gotten in touch with God, but had become God. Words could not describe this new experience...

The previous chapters described the situation, the people, and the tools to create sustainable change in order to have a more satisfying and meaningful life as a self-actualized being. The warriors described in the earlier chapters could be anyone who resonates with the words in any of the chapters. The tools discussed can be used by anyone in order to create a more satisfying life.

The Logical Brain Doesn't Have All the Answers

When we think of anything deeply blissful and joyful in our lives, like the first time we truly fell in love, we realize that it was not a rational process to reach that state of nirvana. In fact, it is as if our brain was turned off when it happened. We reserve our logical brains to get us out of the trouble that we believe our hearts led us into. For example, if the blissful love affair ended up in a dysfunctional marriage, then the logical brain kicks in to help us get out. We might even blame ourselves for not using our brain in the first place when we fell in love. But what a boring and mechanical life it would be if we were always logical and rational. There would be no room for magic.

In my own personal life, when some seemingly bad thing has happened, it has always been for the good of the whole me. This is not something that my brain can comprehend on an intellectual level. Our brains are machines that use logic and rational thinking to get us from point A to point B. When you tap into multidimensional knowledge, which is what you can do when you are wholly integrated, you can go anywhere you choose to go in the moment. It doesn't have to start in the beginning or from point A. It could go from F to Q in one step, and it doesn't have to make any logical sense. Life then becomes magical!

> **Magic is available for those who recognize that there is more to them than the 3-D physical matter that they see in the mirror.**

Magic is available for those who recognize that there is more to them than the 3-D physical matter that they see in the mirror. During all my coaching sessions with many diverse clients, I find confirmation time and again that deep satisfaction and contentment have nothing to do with logic or thinking. In fact, the moment that thinking, analyzing and categorizing creep into our conversation or recollection of true bliss and satisfaction is the moment the magic has left the room. It is as if we are back watching an old black-and-white movie on an antiquated analog television set.

If you want to experience deep satisfaction and bliss, you have to be willing to be open to the possibility that there is more to you than what you see with your eyes and what can be seen with someone else's eyes on an autopsy table. When you feel into this possibility is when magic becomes accessible, and logic is reserved for solving problems like, "where did I leave my keys?" And even the logical types of problems seem to resolve themselves effortlessly.

Disconnect in Order to Connect

It may seem counter-intuitive to think that being detached or disconnected from the details of our lives can actually add depth to our experience, but it does. True satisfaction is not derived from a mental exercise. When we get tangled up in details and drama, we rely on our ability to analyze or our brain to get us out. Unfortunately, it does the opposite. Our logical brain is determined to stay in charge, and will create an even more tangled mess to do so. Soon our emotions kick in, and we are right smack in the middle of drama.

Imagine having a conversation with a five-year-old child about her day. She will go on and on, jumping from one detail on to the next. Sometimes she might even get distracted and change the subject altogether. As an adult, you might find this endearing or cute. However, when conversations with adults your own age feel like the conversation with a five-year-old, you might get frustrated or tune out altogether.

Unfortunately, many adults think in the same disjointed and detail-obsessed way. If you truly choose to stay on the spiritual path towards self-actualization, then you may have to walk away from these types of conversations. Your departure is not about being conceited or thinking that you are better than them. It is about honoring their choice to remain mentally involved and engaged in the 3-D world.

Detachment is not about disengaging. It is about engaging with your whole being, not just your head. Detachment allows you the freedom to choose. Once you start choosing for yourself from a disconnected place, you'll actually find yourself connected to all that is. This is what I call having a true spiritual experience. When you choose with your whole being, not just your head, or from a desperate place, life starts making sense. It makes sense not in the old way that it used to. It is not logical sense that I am writing about. It makes sense in an intuitive and holistic way. You start experiencing deep understandings that you cannot even explain with words. Without self-righteousness, blame, guilt, or shame, everything falls into place and it all seems so effortless.

This path is not for the faint of heart. Letting go is not easy. We have built our entire identity based on clinging to illusions and belief systems. We only know how to hold on. What this path asks of us is to let go of it all. Without the certainty that there will be anything at the end, it can only be done with true self-trust. The self in self-trust is body, mind, heart and spirit acting as one, integrated you.

Spiritual Coaching

This book was written with my spiritual coaching hat on. I am a bicultural woman with a Ph.D. in a scientific field who started questioning things at an early age, but did something about it before I turned 40. I discovered my own core values and realized that I was not living a congruent life. Change was something that I was familiar with, and even with that familiarity, my journey was still extremely difficult.

I wanted to write this book partly because I wanted to tell my own story in hopes that what I have learned might help someone else. I know from my own experience that if you know that someone else has walked on the path that you desire to walk, it gives you some reassurance that you too can do it.

I also wanted to use this opportunity to really explain what it is that I teach my clients. I've always been interested in what motivates people, and digging deep into my own consciousness, psyche, and what I have learned, has brought me to the words printed on these pages. I am a firm believer that I have nothing of real value to offer anyone if I have not walked a mile in their shoes. So if you find my story or my words familiar, chances are we are walking together on the same path.

Please stay a while, read the whole book, and try out the tools and techniques that have worked for me. They are not unique in that I have not invented them. Many of the tools and ideas that I have written about come from other spiritual and metaphysical ideas, concepts, books, and the ideas of great teachers. What might be unique is the order and collection of the tools and ideas and how I've related them to the experiences of being a high-achieving, bicultural woman in my own words. Once again, if you relate to the language, the tone, and the style of this book, then please invest the time in yourself to practice what you have read. It works. I know that it works, because I've tried it and it worked for me.

In spiritual coaching, the client learns to access her whole self through detachment from discontinued, or soon to be discontinued, belief systems. Space is created where there was once little to none, and now there is room to breathe. Like a new baby, the client now is free to re-write her own story by creating her own life through real choice. It sounds simple, yet it can be difficult, which is the reason I recommend not doing it alone. The support and wisdom of a good spiritual coach will help your spiritual evolution.

A spiritual coach is not a guru. A spiritual coach will not do the work for you. A spiritual coach creates the space for discovery to happen. The client is in charge at all times. The client does all the work. The coach creates the safe space for the client to let go and teaches tools to help the client practice being her new integrated self. That is how it works for my clients and me.

Review

Let's revisit the story: *Nothing had really changed in her outer world. She still had the same issues with her family, her job, her friends, etc. However, she felt different inside. She didn't feel like any of her issues were real. There was this other dimension in which she seemed to go into where nothing really mattered because nothing seemed real. She was afraid of losing her intensity. After all, she loved the highs in her life even though, she hated the lows. She couldn't imagine life without intense joy. But it wasn't about joy or sadness anymore. It was about feeling complete. She was complete and as such, didn't need anything or anyone else to fill her up. She felt like she had not just gotten in touch with God, but had become God. Words could not describe this new experience…*

The NEW Un-filtered Conversation: This is for you to create. What is your new un-filtered conversation after reading this book? How would you like to relate to you?

Exercise:

1. Is there anything that you'd like to do differently? What and how would you do them differently?
2. How do you feel after reading this book?
3. What is one thing you'd like to commit to doing or trying after reading this book? How committed are you to doing it?
4. Now that you have read the entire book, do you have any unanswered questions? If so, please contact me via email at sherry@icreateaspace.com. I'd love to talk to you.

Acknowledgements

A very special thank you goes to my parents, Dolly and Goshtasb, who were courageous enough to leave their homeland with two suitcases and no plans except to provide an opportunity for an education for me. I owe everything to them.

Many thanks to my family, Mike, Adam, and Siena, who had to wonder what I was doing on the computer all the time. Thanks for your patience when asked to provide feedback even when you did not want to, and for all your help. Charlie, our pug, was also a key element in maintaining my drive throughout the writing process as he sat next to me quietly and not so quietly (when he was snoring) during much of the writing.

A special acknowledgment goes to my dear friend, Elaine who has been my companion and sounding board throughout my journey of spiritual and personal discovery. Carla and Dave, thanks for teaching me so much.

I also owe much of my inspiration and spiritual guidance to the *Crimson Circle* community, a place where creativity is always nurtured and encouraged. Much of Chapter 5 would not have been possible had it not been for what I learned from the teachers at the *Crimson Circle.*

This book would still be sitting in a folder on my laptop had it not been for the hard work, encouragement, and faith of Kimberly White, my editor and friend.

Last, but not least, is my acknowledgment of and all the bicultural women whose stories touched and inspired me to write. They were friends, coaching clients, and friends of clients who have openly shared their experiences and reconfirmed mine in the process.

www.ingramcontent.com/pod-product-compliance
Lightning Source LLC
LaVergne TN
LVHW051501070426
835507LV00022B/2879